LIFE DURING THE INDUSTRIAL REVOLUTION

LIFE DURING THE INDUSTRIAL REVOLUTION

Reader's
Digest

Published by

THE READER'S DIGEST ASSOCIATION LIMITED

London   New York   Sydney
Montreal   Cape Town

HEAVY DUTY An ironworks in Belgium, the second nation to industrialise.

LOW OVERHEADS
An English seller
of top hats
working door to
door in the 1870s.

CITY AND
COUNTRY Carts
bring food from
the surrounding
countryside
into the market
at Les Halles
in Paris.

LIFE DURING THE INDUSTRIAL REVOLUTION
Edited and designed by Toucan Books Limited
Sole author: Richard Tames

First edition copyright © 1995
The Reader's Digest Association Limited,
Berkeley Square House, Berkeley Square, London W1X 6AB

Reprinted 1996

Copyright © 1995
Reader's Digest Association Far East Limited
Philippines copyright © 1995
Reader's Digest Association Far East Limited

Printing and binding: Printer Gráfica S.A., Barcelona
Separations: Typongraph, Verona, Italy
Paper: Perigord-Condat, France

ISBN 0 276 42126 4

Page 1: Engraving on a share certificate for the
Stockton and Darlington Railway, 1821.

Pages 2-3: 'Ironworks'. Part of a painting by von
Menzel, 1875.

Front cover (clockwise from top left): Old-clothes
seller, 1888; household soap, 1894; London slum,
1889; chimney sweeps, Whitby, 1890s; second-hand
furniture shop, London, 1877; tin of *petits pois*, 1890s;
domestic science class, London, 1908; American
housekeeper's almanac, 1858.

Back cover: Trevithick's portable steam engine, 1908;
Le Petit Journal, 1895; folding push-chair, 1880s;
advertisement for Lipton's Teas, 1880s; women
factory-workers, Germany, 1890s; London firm of
Silber & Fleming, 1880s.

FACTORY GIRLS PREPARING THE WARP FOR THE WEAVER.
"DRAWING IN."

MODEL MANUFACTURERS
Massachusetts mill
girls earned a
reputation for
intelligence and thrift.

TREVITHICKS,
PORTABLE STEAM ENGINE.

Catch me who can.

Mechanical Power Subduing
Animal Speed.

PATHFINDER The first
lumbering colliery
engines were soon
improved until they
could outrun the
fastest horse.

CONTENTS

LOCK AND KEY The Englishman Joseph Bramah
invented this patent lock.

WOMEN'S WORK Textiles
employed more female
labour than any other
branch of industry.

ON THE WAGON An English
chimneysweep has a chat.

A WORLD TRANSFORMED

Starting in Britain in the mid 18th century, the Industrial Revolution transformed the world

and the way in which millions of people lived. Its effects were more revolutionary than any other

development in human history since the discovery of agriculture more than 5000 years ago.

THE INDUSTRIAL Revolution created the way in which most people in the developed world now live – in cities rather than villages, relying for almost all their everyday necessities not upon what they or their neighbours grow or make for themselves, but on large and intricate organisations, staffed by people they will never know or see.

It started in Britain in the mid 18th century as a clutch of enterprising businessmen and engineers discovered new ways of harnessing water and later steam power and of organising their workforces. By the mid 19th century, it had transformed British society. What took Britain a century to achieve took half that time in Germany and the United States in the 19th century and has been achieved in a decade or so in many countries since World War II. For the Industrial Revolution is still with us, still changing the daily lives of millions of people in all parts of the world, bringing misery and upheaval to many, great profits to the lucky or enterprising few. In the long run, it has raised living standards enormously. However, these advantages have usually taken a long time to materialise. During most of the early stages of the Industrial Revolution, which lasted until the outbreak of World War I in 1914, those who benefited most were the rapidly growing middle classes and skilled workers.

But even the lives of ordinary workers and their families were radically changed, as patterns of work and trade were transformed and goods came from farther and farther afield. By the 1850s, the worsted

OLD WORLD   Late 19th-century English farm workers pose for the camera – an invention of the industrial age.

NEW WORLD   The village blacksmith is a world away from an industrial forge in France in the 1890s (above). In the same decade, the age of mass production has arrived in force in the Krupps ironworks in Germany (right).

mills of Yorkshire in the North of England – one of the heartlands of the new industrial world – were drawing raw material from areas as far apart as Peru and Australia. At that time, people living in poor cottages in remote areas, from the islands of Orkney off Scotland to Ontario in Canada, treated machine-made goods and tropical foods such as tea and sugar as novelties; they would soon become necessities. By the 1870s, cowboys from Texas would drive cattle to railheads in Kansas, for their meat to be canned in Chicago and consumed in Cornwall. By the 1880s, people in Canterbury, England, could sit down to a Sunday lunch of roast mutton raised on the plains around Canterbury, New Zealand.

Production and consumption, art and education,

leisure and crime, religion and politics: none would escape the transformation that industry brought in its train. It affected the landscape and environment, too, notably in a gradual but continuous decline in the proportion of people who earned their living by agriculture – from 80 per cent or more in the majority of countries in the 18th century to under 5 per cent in many countries today. The close association with the earth and the cultivation and care of plants and animals that had dominated human existence for millenia was brought to an end. The countryside, once nearly everybody's home, became a sparsely populated and highly efficient food factory, a focus for nostalgia but no longer a source of livelihood for the majority of people.

PASSING ON SKILLS

Ordinary working people helped to spread industry. During the 19th century many English coalminers went to work in Belgium, France and Germany where they passed on their skills to their continental fellows.

They might still take a great interest in the weather and the passage of the seasons, but such rhythms of nature no longer dominated their daily lives.

BREAKING THE ENERGY BARRIER

The preindustrial world was tied to 'natural' forms of energy – the muscle-power of humans and beasts, and the force of wind and water where these could be harnessed. However stupendous the construction of Stonehenge, the Pyramids at Giza, the Roman road system and the temple complexes of ancient Greece, India and Central America, there were limits to what gangs of slaves and teams of animals could do, even when driven to their limits. People had to be fed and protected from disease, and they had to rest, which meant repeated changeovers from one team to the next. Working conditions like these could never provide the focused, flexible power required by modern industry.

That is why the invention of steam power lay at the heart of the Industrial Revolution. Even the first generation of crude pumping engines, generating only tens of horsepower, were tireless in operation and compact enough to work at the bottom of a mine shaft, where 500 horses could never have been accommodated, let alone coordinated. Horses, moreover, consume the produce of the land – thus competing with humans – whereas engines consume coal, which in the 18th century seemed to be a more or less limitless new source of energy.

The earliest engines were not 'fuel-efficient' by modern standards, yielding about 1 per cent of input as output, compared with 10-20 per cent for humans or animals. But the land could never have

IRONBRIDGE   A carriage crosses the world's first cast-iron bridge, built over the River Severn in Shropshire in 1779. The bridge was cast locally at Coalbrookdale, as were the world's first railway wheels and rails.

WILLIAM MACKENZIE: GIANT OF THE RAILWAYS

BLASTING A CUTTING
Whole landscapes were transformed by the railways.

FORGOTTEN GENIUS
Attention to detail – shown in these diagrams – was the secret of pioneers such as William Mackenzie.

A S THE Industrial Revolution spread, so did the railways, crisscrossing continents and countries, and shrinking the globe in their iron embrace. They transformed the landscape, too. Starting in Britain but soon moving out across Europe, North America and the rest of the world, teams of skilled engineers and labourers (known in Britain as 'navvies') bored tunnels through hills and mountains, raised embankments and viaducts, and built bridges across rivers and estuaries –

many of them feats of engineering that dwarfed even the Pyramids of the ancient Egyptian pharaohs in their scale and ambition.

The men who organised these titanic undertakings were aware of their own heroic stature, but some made more of a mark on the landscape than on posterity. In Britain, for example, the associates of William Mackenzie (1794-1851) included figures such as the father-and-son team George and Robert Stephenson (responsible for the pioneering steam locomotive *Rocket* among many projects), Thomas Telford (the Scottish engineer who built the Menai Bridge linking Anglesey with the mainland of North Wales) and Thomas Brassey (builder of railways in regions as diverse as

the Crimea in Russia, Canada and South America). These men are remembered, but Mackenzie himself has been all but forgotten in his country – perhaps because he devoted much of his later career to contracting overseas.

The self-taught son of a canal contractor, Mackenzie was one of the most remarkable entrepreneurs of his age, building tunnels, viaducts, docks, bridges, stations and even an asylum. In Britain, his major works included the Liverpool and Manchester Railway, as well as the Birmingham Canal. Elsewhere, he rendered navigable 200 miles (320 km) of the River Shannon in Ireland, built nine major railways in France and two in Spain and dug a canal to link the Rhine and Marne rivers. His other business interests included numerous ironworks in France and property developments in his native Lancashire. He died comparatively young at the age of 57. Even so, the contracts he had been involved in during his lifetime were valued at £17 million – a colossal sum at the time.

MOTOR OF INDUSTRY
A German steam turbine of around 1900 is a far cry from the first steam engines of the late 18th century.

And it was no accident that the world's first industrial powerhouses grew up on or near large coalfields – in South Wales and on Tyneside in northern England, in eastern Pennsylvania and in the Ruhr Valley in Germany.

THE BRITISH DIFFERENCE
Historians, explaining why Britain led the world into industry, have concentrated on what the country could supply. Britain had large deposits of coal, iron, copper, lead and tin, conveniently located near each other, near the surface and near navigable waterways allowing them to be transported easily. Furthermore, the ingenious British invented new machines and techniques that allowed these materials to be exploited on an unprecedented scale and to be made into novel products and distributed by new methods – by canal, along artificially surfaced roads and, a generation later, by railway and steamship.

produced the food and fodder to sustain the people and beasts needed to power the industries Britain went on to create. By 1870 Britain's steam-engine capacity was about 4 million horsepower, equivalent to the power that could be generated by 40 million adult males – at a time when the British population had only about a quarter that many grown men.

No industrial miracle could have happened without steam power.

The other force that drove the industrial revolution was demand. What set Britain apart from the rest of Europe was a buoyant and expanding market. As early as the 1720s, Daniel Defoe – an unsinkable entrepreneur, as well as creator of *Robinson Crusoe*, who claimed to have made and lost a dozen fortunes – recognised this: 'Even those we call poor

LAMBETH WALK In pre-industrial times, children danced round the village Maypole. Here, in the 1890s, they dance to the sound of the barrel organ in the streets of London.

NEW TIMES, NEW POWER
Steam powered the factories of Springfield, Massachusetts, in the 1870s. By 1913, gas turbines were making an appearance, as in this German factory.

people, journeymen, working and painstaking people do thus: they lie warm, live in plenty, work hard and know no want. 'Tis for these your markets are kept open late on Saturday nights, because they usually receive their week's wages late . . . in a word, these are the life of our whole commerce.'

Large and populous France might dazzle the rest of Europe with the grandeur of its palaces, the number of its cathedrals and the size of its armies – but all these represented a burden on its grumbling middle classes and groaning peasantry. If the country was wealthy, its people were not. Harvest failures could still cause death by famine in France in the last quarter of the 18th century, 150 years after the last such disaster in mainland Britain. The 18th-century English labourer despised his Gallic counterpart because he wore wooden shoes and ate black bread. An Englishman ate white, wheaten bread and was shod with leather.

Britain's middle classes were an ever-growing market for the output of new industries. They wanted to dress as well as they ate, to paper their walls, carpet their floors and fill their rooms with solid, well-made furnishings, pots and clocks, lamps and crockery. They made their country the world's first consumer society. In his *Instructions for Travellers*, the clergyman Dean Tucker boasted in 1758 that Britain was: 'A free country, where riches got by trade are no disgrace, and where property is also safe . . . and where every person may make what display he pleases of his wealth. . . .'

A decade later, another observer argued that the openness of English society, compared with caste-ridden Europe, promoted a taste for novelty that was a great encouragement to new businesses: 'In England the several ranks of men slide into each other almost imperceptibly . . . Hence arises a strong emulation in all the several stations and conditions to vie with each other; and a perpetual restless ambition in each of the inferior ranks to raise themselves to the level of those immediately above them. In such a state as this fashion must have an uncontrolled sway. And a fashionable luxury must spread through it like a contagion.'

The 'fashionable luxuries' of the 1760s, such as tea and china cups to drink it from, had become common comforts half a century later. The potter Josiah Wedgwood was a striking example of the market-led approach to manufacturing that helped

PALACE OF COMMERCE Handsome London headquarters testify to the prosperity of import-export firm Silber and Fleming, founded in 1856. Trading across the globe, their stock ranged from meat grinders to garden tools, tents to porcelain.

retained a strength unknown in Britain, controlling prices and technologies, and restricting the movement of workers and money. Freedom, energy and an alertness to market opportunities became the keys to British success, as a Parliamentary Committee noted with smug satisfaction in 1806: 'The rapid and prodigious increase of late years in the manufactures and commerce of this country is universally known . . . [It] is principally to be ascribed to the general spirit of enterprise and industry among a free and enlightened people, left to the unrestrained exercise of their talents in the employment of a vast capital. . . .'

Foreign markets provided another stimulus. As a seafaring nation that traded with almost every part of the globe, Britain was well placed to take advantage of new markets, wherever they presented themselves. Once again, Wedgwood is an example of the globally minded marketeer. He produced catalogues of his wares in foreign languages, with prices in foreign currencies. Concerned that 'every gentle and

COMFORT FOR BABIES From cradle to grave, people benefited from the products of industry.

industry to thrive. He lavished care and expenditure on producing goods of the highest standard, knowing that he could be sure of recouping his money by subsequently reproducing them much more cheaply for the mass market.

THE GLOBAL MARKETPLACE

Britain was the largest free-trade area in all Europe. Throughout the European mainland, tolls and tariffs doubled and trebled and quadrupled the price of goods moving across city or regional boundaries. Guilds of merchants and craftsmen

WARES OF INDUSTRY **London's Great Exhibition of 1851 set the trend for a series of international exhibitions.**

decent push should be made to have our things seen and sold at foreign markets', he gave departing British ambassadors entire dinner services to use for their official entertaining. He sent a thousand parcels, containing £20 000 worth of pottery, to the minor nobility of Europe to try to repeat his successful domestic strategy of starting at the top of the social pyramid and working downwards. He also understood that each foreign market had its own particular tastes and needs: intricate decoration for

DANGEROUS PLACE TO LIVE

London in the 18th century was a very unhealthy place to live. During the period of 100 years, afflictions such as tuberculosis and epidemic outbreaks such as typhoid carried off at least 600 000 of its population. As a result, the city needed large numbers of migrants coming in from country towns and villages to help it to stay the same size.

France, where the delicate ornamentation of rococo taste prevailed long after it had faded in England; for Russia, 'showy, tawdry, cheap things, cover'd all over with colours'; and for the American colonies, cheap, sturdy wares and 'seconds'.

By the beginning of the 19th century, the first phase of the Industrial Revolution had created new patterns of commerce across the world in which objects of daily consumption, such as cutlery or cotton cloth, could be traded over vast distances. The second phase, which featured a transport revolution using railways and steamships, meant that even raw materials, such as grain and timber could also be exchanged profitably across continents.

PROPHET OF OPTIMISM

Possibly the most influential writer of the newly industrial world was not Charles Darwin (pioneer of evolutionary theory) or Karl Marx (co-author of the *Communist Manifesto*) but Samuel Smiles, who outsold even the novelist Charles Dickens. A Scot by

TRAVEL IN THE **1890**S **A French lady and her child wait for a train. Luxury dining is part of the service in Pullman cars.**

birth, Smiles had qualified as a doctor by the age of 20, but abandoned medicine for journalism and then moved into management in the railway industry. After giving a series of lectures on self-improvement to an audience of young men in Leeds, Smiles went on to publish these lectures in book form in 1859 as *Self-Help, with Illustrations of Character and Conduct*. By the end of the century *Self-Help* had sold over a quarter of a million copies and had been translated into every major European language, and several Asian ones as well.

If the creators of the new industrial order put their faith in 'the gospel of work', *Self-Help* was its testament. Its central message, repeated with a wealth of biographical examples by way of 'proof',

was that any man of ordinary abilities could, by steady effort and self-education, make his way to success. The message was eagerly listened to on both sides of the Channel, both sides of the Atlantic, and both sides of the globe. The endeavour and need for sheer effort that Smiles confidently preached was an essential ingredient in the Industrial Revolution. What its critics derided as 'steam intellect' was as crucial for industry as the steam engine.

IN JAPAN Building a railway network was a key part of Japan's modernising drive, starting in the 1860s.

THE NEW WORLD OF WORK

The Industrial Revolution's new technologies, based on water and
steam power, created new skills as they destroyed old ones. Factory, foundry,
mill and mine, each evolved its own complex hierarchy, based on ownership,
expertise, dexterity or danger. While work was elevated to the level of an
ethical principle, the very notion of craftsmanship was endangered and
workers reduced to the level of mere 'hands'.

IN FACTORY AND FOUNDRY

Although small-scale workshops increased in numbers, production in the new growth

industries was increasingly dominated by factories – large-scale concentrations

of labour where the rhythm of work was set by machines.

DANIEL DEFOE, sometime pamphleteer, government agent, businessman and author of *Robinson Crusoe,* wrote a vivid account of the traditional cloth-making districts of the West Riding of Yorkshire, England, in the 1720s: 'The nearer we came to Halifax, we found the houses thicker, and the villages greater in every bottom [valley] . . . In short . . . we found the country one continued village . . . hardly an house standing out of a speaking distance from another: and . . . we could see at every house a tenter [frame], and on almost every tenter a piece of cloth.'

The ever-observant Defoe noted that each cloth-worker's cottage had access to a running stream, essential for washing and dyeing his wool, and that each cottage garden was manured by the dung of a cow, kept for its milk, and a horse, which

CRAFTSMAN'S ICON A porcelain milkmaid, hand-made for Catherine the Great of Russia, is an example of craftsmanship before the age of mass production.

the clothier needed for his weekly trip to market to sell his finished piece and buy more wool and provisions.

A gratifying scene of industriousness spread out on either side of the traveller: 'Though we met few people without doors [that is, outside], yet within we saw the houses full . . . all employed from the youngest to the oldest; scarce any thing above four years old, but its hands were sufficient for its own support. Nor a beggar to be seen . . . The people in general live long; they enjoy a good air; and under such circumstances hard labour is naturally attended with the blessing of health, if not riches.' *(continued on page 20)*

PRODUCTS AND POLLUTION Customers of a mid-19th-century Danish retailer of household textiles and carpets (right) benefit from the improved productivity of Britain's export industries. In England, Bradford in 1873 pays the polluted price of progress (below).

FROM FOOD TO CARS: THE ASSEMBLY LINE

THE ASSEMBLY LINE is the child of the food-processing industries. One of its earliest appearances was in the fully automated flour mill patented by the American Oliver Evans in 1790. Powered entirely by water and gravity, Evans's automatic mill incorporated all three main types of conveyor mechanism (belt, bucket and screw) to grind some 300 bushels (385 cu ft – 11 m³) of grain an hour with an overall labour saving of 50 per cent. In 1805 Evans went on to adapt his continuous bucket chain to create a steam-powered dredger.

A less sophisticated operation was established in 1804 at the British Royal Navy Victualling Office, Deptford, where five bakers, each specialising in a single operation, produced ship's biscuits at the rate of 70 a minute. By the 1830s, the process had been fully mechanised, with trays of biscuits conveyed from mixing machine to rollers to cutter to oven on continuously moving roller-beds. By the 1850s, there were continuous-flow systems of baking bread, drying fruit and canning fruit and vegetables. In the 1860s, American slaughterhouses introduced the overhead rail systems pioneered in Manchester 30 years before.

The assembly line achieved its ultimate form, however, in the moving-track automobile-assembly system introduced by Henry Ford at Highlands Park, Michigan, in 1913, which reduced the time per chassis from 728 minutes to 93.

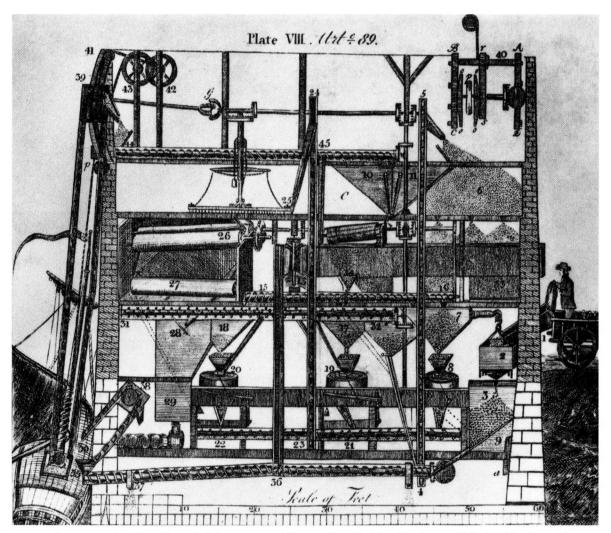

LABOUR SIDELINED In Oliver Evans's fully automated flour mill, at Redclay Creek near Philadelphia, the worker was only required to feed in the raw material and carry away the finished product.

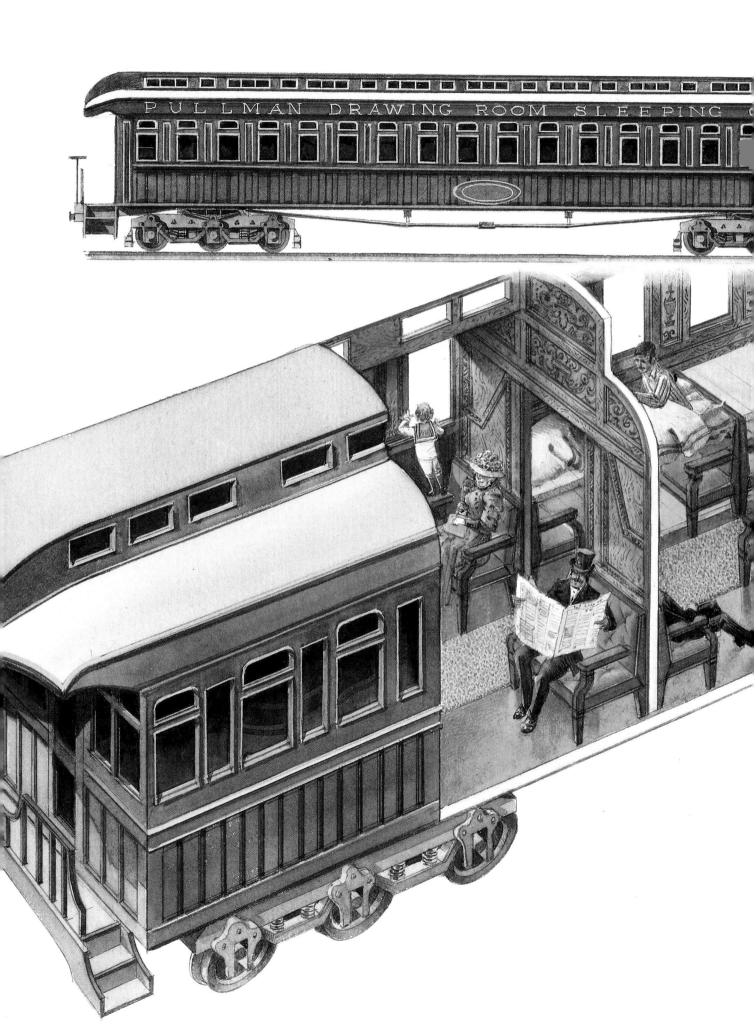

PULLMAN LUXURY

ADVANCES in engineering and manufacturing permitted new luxury in travel. For those who could afford it, the American industrialist George Pullman offered railroad cars that reproduced many home comforts, including areas for sleeping, dining and socialising. He is said to have had the idea for his 'sleepers' as a prospector in Colorado in 1859 when he saw miners sleeping in double-decked bunks.

In 1867 he founded Pullman's Palace Car Company in Chicago, manufacturing cars and running services across the United States. Six years later he shipped 18 cars to Britain, introducing Pullman comfort to the British and later continental European railways.

TRAPPINGS OF LUXURY George Pullman points out the benefits of his patent Allen Paper Wheel, one of many devices that improved the comfort of his luxury railroad cars.

Such semi-industrialised countryside was unusual in 18th-century Europe, but it was not unique. The Austrian Imperial Woollen Factory employed 750 workers in Linz, the focal point of its operations, and 26 000 home-based workers scattered throughout the hills of Upper Austria, Bohemia and Moravia. At the French state sail-making factory in Anvers, 642 workers were employed full-time, while ten times as many worked part-time in the countryside round about.

In 1748, Frederick the Great of Prussia ordered his peasantry to pay a special tax, not in coin, but in linen yarn. This would not only supply shirts for his soldiers but stop farmers and their children spending 'the long evenings of the autumn and winter in idleness'. By devoting those hours to spinning and weaving, they would also 'raise themselves by it, as well as getting used to habits of industry, inasmuch as the laziness of our subjects . . . is the only reason why they find themselves in straitened circumstances'.

Organising for Output

The 'putting-out' system revolved around a 'master', who gave credit or materials to semi-independent craftsmen, working in their own homes or attached premises, to turn, for example, yarn into cloth or iron rods into nails. Their output was then returned to him to sell on to wholesalers, to retailers or directly to consumers. This system demanded considerable managerial skills on the part of the 'master'. On the other hand, it required him to supervise only the quality of the final product, not the process of manufacture. To that extent, at least, the man who wove the cloth still 'owned' his work as well as his tools. Such men were paid by the 'piece', not the hour, and worked hard or not as they chose.

Cloth-makers, potters and metal-workers all regularly kept 'St Monday' – that is, they kept Monday as a holiday. To shoemakers it was 'St Crispin', to woolcombers 'St Blaise' and to smiths 'St Clement'. For all of them, it was a day for drinking away the earnings of the previous week, playing cards or skittles and pottering in their gardens. Tuesday was often a hangover day, when the pace of work was necessarily slow. From Wednesday to Saturday the pace became increasingly frantic until the deadline for a completed piece or batch was met and the cycle began again.

A major step towards efficiency, which started to happen in Britain around the mid 18th century, was to centralise production under the supervision of an entrepreneur, who determined not only what was made but when and how. Even without steam power, the factory was an organisational revolution as profound as the technological transformations that so impressed contemporary observers. The full-blooded transition to mechanised industrial production did not take place outside Britain and Belgium until after 1850. But the crucial organisational breakthrough was made a century before, not in textiles, Europe's biggest industry, but in such industries as ceramics and metalwares. Its pioneers were British, figures such as Josiah Wedgwood and Matthew Boulton, business partner to the inventor James Watt.

Wedgwood was working in an industry buoyed up by rising demand – caused partly by the rise in numbers and incomes of the 'middling sort' in England, and partly by the shift from pewter to pottery as hot tea and coffee displaced ale as the

REWARDS OF LABOUR English shoemakers 'honour' St Crispin's Day in 1836 at the appropriately named 'Blue Last'. On the right, a drunken bootmaker beats his wife.

BYWORD FOR TASTE Josiah Wedgwood (above left) was a businessman, artist, scientist and philanthropist. His factory Etruria (above) stood by the Trent and Mersey Canal, which provided cheap transport for clay and a smooth way of carrying away his delicate products. Left: A 'thrower' and his assistant around 1890.

daily beverage of all classes. Although porcelain factories had been established under royal patronage in continental Europe – at Meissen in Saxony (in 1710) and at Sèvres in France (1756) – the typical producer in the mid 18th century was still a master potter who might employ one or two members of his own family, but increasingly needed to recruit journeymen and apprentices from outside the ranks of his relatives. Despite the increase in scale from family to workshop, the old work habits prevailed, with regular one, two or even three-day stoppages for a fair, a funeral or a drinking bout.

Wedgwood's model factory, 'Etruria', built in Staffordshire in 1769 at the junction of a

newly made road and a newly dug canal, reflected the shift in control of production from man to master. Each worker was assigned to a department which specialised in a particular type of ware – jasper or basalt, 'ornamental' or 'useful'. By 1790 the 'useful' department employed 160 people, who were engaged in more than 20 tasks, as 'throwers', 'turners', 'pressers', 'dippers', 'brushers', 'placers', 'colour-grinders', 'painters', 'modellers' and so on. No longer did a single person make a single product from beginning to end.

Wedgwood trained his workers to become skilled – but on his own terms. These skills were limited. Workers were paid by the hour, not the piece, and summoned to work by a bell. Output was measured closely and a hierarchy of wage rates calculated. By the early 1790s weekly wages at Etruria ranged from 1s (5 pence) for a boy who helped to handle horses to 42s (£2.10) for a skilled hand-painter

CONSUMING PASSION This earthenware tea service of 1845 was designed by Henry Cole, chief organiser of London's Great Exhibition of 1851.

KING COTTON The sheer size of cotton mills in Manchester (above) impressed contemporaries in 1829. The yarn spinning machine (right) patented by Richard Arkwright in 1769 was probably not his own invention – but he successfully exploited it, ending up with a fortune and a knighthood.

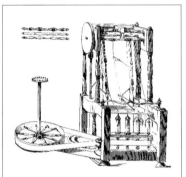

(the price of a loaf of bread at this time varied between about 6d and 1s 6d). Wedgwood gave strict instructions that unpunctuality was to be punished by the loss of earnings: 'Those who come later than the hour appointed should be noticed, and if after repeated marks of disapprobation they do not come in due time, an account of the time they are deficient in should be taken, and so much of their wages stopt as the time comes to.'

Half a century later, factory hands would routinely be locked out if they were more than five minutes late, losing half a day's pay and paying a fine on top of that to compensate the employer for 'loss of steam'. Evidence from a Massachusetts engineering shop shows an even greater tightening of the screw: 'During working hours the men are not allowed to speak to each other, though working close together, on pain of instant discharge. Men are hired to watch and patrol the shop.' What made this oppression possible? A letter from an emigrant to America, a former Sheffield cutler, to his old workmates, provides a clue: 'Men never learn to do a knife through, as they do in Sheffield. The knives go through 40 or 50 hands.'

A young machinist, giving evidence before a US Senate Committee in 1883, described the progress of what would now be called 'de-skilling' throughout the engineering industry: 'The trade has been subdivided and those subdivisions have again been subdivided, so that a man never learns the . . . trade now . . . One man may make just a particular part of a machine and may not know anything whatever about another part of the same machine. In that way machinery is produced a great deal cheaper than it used to be . . . and in fact, through this system of work, 100 men are able to do now what it took 300 or 400 men to do 15 years ago . . . There is no system of apprenticeship . . . You simply go in and learn whatever branch you are put at and you stay at that unless you are changed to another. . . .'

The same witness went on to complain that the system had 'a very demoralising effect upon the mind throughout. The man . . . knows he cannot

FLYING SHUTTLE Looms which propelled the shuttle across the weft by means of hammers made it possible to weave cloth that was wider than the weaver's own reach.

A SOUTH CAROLINA COTTON MILL IN 1903

THE SOCIAL investigator Marie Van Vorst found grim conditions in a South Carolina cotton mill:
❛ The air of the room is white with cotton, although the spool-room is perhaps the freest. These little particles are breathed into the nose, drawn into the lungs. Lung disease and pneumonia are the constant, never-absent scourge of the mill-village. The girls expectorate to such an extent that the floor is nauseous with it . . . When the people are ill they are docked for wages. When, for indisposition or fatigue, they knock a day off, there is a man hired especially for this purpose, who rides from house to house to find out what is the matter with them, to urge them to rise, and if they are not literally too sick to move, they are hounded out of their beds and back to their looms. ❜

MINDING MACHINES The advanced spinning technology of the 1830s required fewer attendants. A child on the right of the picture crawls under the moving machine to sweep up waste.

leave that particular branch and go to any other; he has got no chance whatever to learn anything else because he is kept steadily and constantly at that particular thing'.

The cotton industry was the first to mechanise production fully and to switch from water to steam power and from country to town locations. The pioneer British firms were in Derbyshire and Nottingham-shire, Wales and Scotland, often in remote areas, where fast-flowing streams provided their power, via huge water wheels. This was why the buildings that housed their machinery came to be known as 'mills' – a name that stuck after they had switched to steam power.

Recruiting labour proved difficult. The mills themselves loomed grim and alien in the land-scape, looking to most ordinary working folk like prisons or fortresses, an impression confirmed by the decision of Richard Arkwright, inventor of the 'water frame' spinning machine, to install a battery of cannon to defend his six-storey mill at Cromford, after another of his mills, near Chorley, had been attacked and destroyed by a mob during a trade depression in 1779.

WOOING THE WORKERS

Employers placed enticing advertisements to woo new hands, particularly women and children, who were cheaper than men as well as more nimble and less likely to cause trouble. One British mill pro-mised parents that their children would be 'well clothed, lodged and boarded . . .'. It added that the children would 'attend church every Sabbath and have proper masters appointed for their instruction'.

However, only one-tenth of the children who

PROGRESSIVE EDUCATION
Children dance the quadrille in the Institute for the Formation of Character at the New Lanark cotton mills of the utopian industrialist Robert Owen.

were employed at Cuckney Mill in Nottinghamshire, England, between 1786 and 1805 were placed there by their families or guardians. The rest came from orphanages, asylums or workhouses for the desperately poor of whom 8 per cent died and 15 per cent simply ran away.

A generation later the British cotton industry had become concentrated around Manchester and Glasgow. By the second decade of the 19th century, when cotton surpassed wool as the leading textile industry in Britain, the country had 200 mills with more than 400 workers and ten with more than 600. Birley's mill at Chorlton on Medlock, for example, consisted of several 'huge buildings, separated from each other by streets, but connected by subterranean tunnels, in which iron tramways are laid down for the speedier and easier conveyance from ware-room to ware-room of the raw material. Nearly 2000 hands are regularly employed in this vast industrial colony'.

The breakneck expansion of the cotton industry so impressed contemporaries that by 1835 it had

SHODDY RAGS

'Shoddy', meaning of the poorest quality, was originally the name given to cloth made from recycled rags and the sweepings of the mill floors.

its own historian, Edward Baines, who exulted in the dazzling achievements of its technology. A single 100 horsepower engine, he informed his readers, had the strength of 880 men and could drive 50 000 spindles simultaneously, producing in a 12 hour shift 62 000 miles (100 000 km) of thread, enough to go right round the Earth two and a half times. Looking back to 1760, when cotton manufacture supported only 40 000 people, Baines calculated that it now supported 1.5 million because 'one spinner can now produce as much yarn in a single

BARE NECESSITIES **Pictures of lodgings for Manchester workers in the 1860s stress their lack of furnishings. Most were cold, draughty and overcrowded as well.**

SALTAIRE: A MODEL COMMUNITY

PATRIARCH Top: Sir Titus Salt (1803-76) served Bradford as Mayor and as a Member of Parliament. His company town Saltaire was dominated by a huge, carefully designed mill, and provided housing for 850 families.

SALTAIRE was built just outside Bradford in the North of England over a period of 20 years. It eventually housed a population of 4500 on a site extending over 49 acres. Its 22 streets were named after the Queen, Prince Albert, the architect employed to build it, his wife, their children and so on. Each of the 850 family dwellings had gas, water, a privy, a coal store and an ashpit for the tidy disposal of the waste from the hearth. There were no policemen, no pawnshops and initially no public houses, since its builder, the industrialist Sir Titus Salt, was a teetotaller who had a sign erected in the town stating: 'Abandon beer all ye who enter here.'

The town's first public building was an Italianate Congregational church capable of accommodating 800 worshippers. Later there was a

RESTRICTED RECREATION Saltaire's large park was closed until 2 pm on Sundays to encourage attendance at worship. Dogs were banned from it.

Methodist chapel and a Sunday School. Other public amenities included baths, wash-houses, a school, a hospital, a library and an 'institute' to serve as 'a public house without its evils': this provided a dignified meeting place for the Pig, Dog, Poultry, Pigeon and Horticultural Societies. In 1871, Salt gave the town a park where cricket could be played, but smoking was forbidden.

À LA MODE A fashion plate of 1862 features Salt's stylish and durable alpaca fabrics.

day as formerly in a year [and] . . . fabrics can be bleached in two days to a pure white that would formerly have required six or eight months'.

At the same time, the insatiable appetites of the new machines sent merchants scouring the world for new sources of raw cotton, and there was a solution to this problem as well. In 1793, the American Eli Whitney had invented the cotton gin which enormously reduced the costs of separating cotton fibres from seeds. Now there was no limit to the supply of raw material as plantations worked by slaves marched across the southern USA from the Atlantic to the Mississippi. Between the 1790s and 1830s, raw cotton exports from America soared from 500 000 to 300 million lb (227 000 to 136 million kg), and the price of cotton plummeted.

The increase in the scale of operations created a gulf between master and man. In the Britain of 1841, Canon Parkinson, author of a pamphlet *On the Present Condition of the Labouring Poor in Manchester*, claimed: 'There is no town in the world where the distance between the rich and the poor is so great . . . There is far less personal communication between the master cotton-spinner and his workmen, between the calico-printer and his blue-handed boys . . . than there is between the Duke of Wellington and the humblest labourer on his estate . . .' A *Morning Chronicle* journalist who visited Manchester in 1849 was told by a 'cardroom hand' – 'I have worked in that mill, sir, these 19 years, and the master never spoke to me once. I think if he did I would be gratified like, and go on working with better heart.' Another opined that this was a deliberate policy, intended to intimidate: 'The masters are afraid that if they speak to us they will be losing their authority; and so they say the overlookers and managers must see to everything.'

Wool followed a generation behind cotton. In the 1830s Yorkshire, the heart of the industry, had only 11 mills with over 200 workers. Other mills – a few hundred of them – employed on average less than a third as many. Saltaire was a model industrial settlement created in the 1850s near the city of Bradford by Sir Titus Salt. This 'Palace of Industry', built in the Italianate style, with a 25 ft (7.6 m) chimney disguised as a campanile bell-tower, covered just under 7 acres (2.8 ha), was six floors high and as long as St Paul's Cathedral in London. The spinning hall on the top floor – 550 ft (168 m) long by 72 ft (22 m) wide – was, at the time of its construction, the largest room in the Western world. In the glass-covered weaving-shed, 1200 looms produced 18 miles (29 km) of cloth each working day.

AN AGE OF IRON

The mechanisation of the textile industries depended, in turn, on the new technologies that had made iron, and later steel, so cheap that it could be substituted for wood in the manufacture of, first, tools, then machines, then rails and, finally, major structures such as cranes, bridges and ships. Without the products of the foundry, the factory – itself an iron-framed building from the 1830s – would not have been possible.

In Britain, the modern metalworking industries developed first in the West Midlands and around the city of Sheffield. Birmingham remained the leader in producing small metalwares, known

NEW SKYLINES Smoke-belching chimneys at Essen in Germany fouled the atmosphere but were a visible guarantee of employment. Crowded industrial sites and neat farmland existed cheek by jowl.

WORK OF GIANTS Kilsby Tunnel, built for the London and Midland Railway in 1839, was a mile (1.6 km) long and cost more than 100 lives. 'Fritz', a steam hammer at the Krupps works at Essen, was used to forge huge steel components for building projects.

generically as 'toys' – such as buttons, buckles, locks, needles, guns and garden tools – while Sheffield specialised in steel, especially cutlery and edged tools. By the 1840s, a Birmingham firm was producing 45 different kinds of axes 'including 14 varieties manufactured expressly for the American market, ornamented with the American eagle, and designated with such names as the Kentucky wedge axe, the American slinging hatchet, the New Orleans axe, etc'. The same firm also offered 70 different types of hoe, each intended for a different type of soil and climate, including those of the Carolinas and around Boston. Most of the fearsome 'Bowie' knives beloved of American frontiersmen were also from Sheffield.

Working conditions in factories were far more likely to brutalise men than to civilise them, and it was therefore with astonishment that a visitor to the Cyfarthfa ironworks in South Wales in the 1840s recorded the existence of a 16-strong brass band, recruited entirely from the foundrymen –

'AN IRON FORGE' Joseph Wright of Derby's painting of 1772 casts industry in a heroic light. The cheap, durable products of the iron industry, such as this ornamental dog and fire grate (far right), helped to fuel a consumer revolution.

'I have seldom heard a regimental band more perfect'. Suddenly he understood 'how to account for hearing . . . the boys in Cyfarthfa works whistling the best airs from the most popular operas'. One advantage of this was that while the men were rehearsing or performing, they had less time for drinking, gambling and fighting.

Working in extreme temperatures and amid toxic gases for 12 hours at a stretch, men – and boys from the age of eight – were liable to heat exhaustion or giddiness, with (continued on page 33)

HEROIC ENGINEERS

'Engineer' once meant a maker of siege towers and catapults. The Industrial Revolution threw engineers into the battle of production.

THE ENGINEERING industry had no single ancestor. Masons and architects, millwrights and wheelwrights, gunsmiths and blacksmiths, makers of clocks and navigational instruments, all in their different ways contributed to its emergence. *Campbell's London Tradesmen*, first published in 1747, explained the requirements for this emerging branch of industry: 'The Engineer makes Engines for raising of Water by Fire, either for supplying Reservoirs or draining Mines . . . The Engineer requires a very mechanically turned head . . . He employs Smiths of various sorts, Founders for his Brass work, Plumbers for his Leadwork, and a Class of Shoe-makers for his

Leather Pipes. He requires a large stock (at least £500) to set up with and a considerable acquaintance among the Gentry . . . He ought to have a solid, not a flighty Head, otherwise his Business will tempt him to many useless and expensive Projects.'

A century later, engineering had come of age as a profession, with a clear professional distinction between civil and mechanical engineers – even if a genius like the British engineer Isambard Kingdom Brunel (builder of the Great Western Railway and the first transatlantic steamship, the *Great Western*) could bestride both worlds. Engineering works had come to specialise in the building

of steam engines, textile machinery, locomotives, agricultural equipment and machine tools, such as lathes and presses. Machines had attained unimagined levels of power and precision. Samuel Smiles, author of the bestselling *Self-Help* (1859), described with admiration how one Joseph Bramah had invented a machine for numbering banknotes, 'a tap wherewith to draw a glass of beer, and . . . a hydraulic machine capable of tearing up a tree by the roots', while James Nasmyth's piledriver could drive a pile in four minutes that would previously have taken 12 hours.

Despite such innovations as the

HORSEPOWER A horse turns the wheels that crush crude metal in an early 18th-century brassworks. Elsewhere, workmen use crank handles and simple levers to mix zinc and copper and cut the finished sheets of brass.

DRAMA AND DISASTER A painting of Coalbrookdale, Shropshire, by the French artist P.J. Loutherbourg, emphasises the spectacular setting of this cradle of heavy industry. Right: Isambard Kingdom Brunel (1803-59) was one of the geniuses of 19th-century engineering.

traction engine and the piledriver, civil engineering and construction remained largely dependent on the pick and shovel, the wheelbarrow and the traditional skills of the mason and bricklayer. Project managers were frequently overwhelmed by the urgency and complexity of their daily tasks and the shortage of competent assistants to whom they could delegate. James Brindley, builder of the pioneering Bridgewater Canal in Lancashire, complained bitterly of having to combine the roles of 'land surveyor, carpenter, mason, brickmaker, boatbuilder, paymaster and engineer', as well as supervising the labours of 600 men. The construction of dykes, docks, canals, turnpike roads, bridges and railways all required the recruitment and supervision of whole armies of 'navvies' (the word comes from 'navigators' – builders of 'navigations', or canals). In building the Great Western Railway, Brunel had to take personal charge of the completion of what his critics called the 'monstrous and extraordinary, most dangerous and impracticable tunnel at Box' (near Bath) when it was already four months past its deadline. Nearly 2 miles (3.2 km) long, it was by far the greatest tunnel ever attempted, and for two and a half years absorbed a ton of gun-powder and a ton of candles every week, not to mention a total of 30 million bricks.

For six months Brunel drove 4000 men and 300 horses to work round the clock. When the tunnel was finally finished in June 1841 the entire route from London to Bristol lay open, but 'the finest work in England' had cost more than twice its original estimate and Box tunnel alone had accounted for more than 100 lives.

WORK OF GIANTS By the time the Blackwall tunnel under the Thames was opened in 1897 deep tunnelling had become routine – but the men behind this project were still evidently in some awe of their own work.

THE CANAL BUILDERS

BRITAIN'S CANALS were built by armies of workers who came to be known as 'navigators' – 'navvies' for short. They used no technology more sophisticated than the pulley block, wheelbarrow, horse-powered hoist (or horse gin) and blasting powder. They also had specialised hand tools for cutting into the earth, shovelling it away, dredging mud and 'puddling' the clay bed of the canal to form an impervious surface. The horse gins hoisted loaded wheelbarrows up inclined barrow runs to cart off the soil. Small kilns (below) burned lime, brought by cart along a plateway, to turn it into mortar. The most expensive part of canal-building was constructing bridges and locks to enable barges to move from one water level to another.

A DYKE-DIGGER IN THE NETHERLANDS

THIS YEAR, 1891, Jan and his brother, Willem, are working on a section of the Merwede Canal in the Netherlands. Last year it was a new harbour; the year before that, restoring a drainage dyke. Jan and Willem are *polderjongens* (polder boys) who specialise in 'ground work' – shifting earth. As younger brothers in a large family they help out on their parents' farm in the off season, but each spring leave their village in Zeeland and head for a major construction project. Here they look for a *putbaas* (pit-boss) putting together a gang to complete a task for which he has been subcontracted.

Each lad comes carrying his own tools and a farm sack. He has his own bedding, spare clothes, cutlery and some provisions from the farm. They will live in a hut, made from a framework of wood, covered in canvas, roofed with reeds and walled with sods. Their cooking and mending will be done by their *keet-vrouw* (shed woman), Beatrix, an unmarried daughter of their *putbaas*, Piet.

The working day begins around 3.30 am. The 14 men in the boys' shed wait their turn to use the *papegaai* (parrot), a pole resting on two wooden stakes over a ditch.

CANAL FISHING   In the low-lying Netherlands, skilled management of waterways and drainage systems was crucial to the nation's prosperity.

This serves as their latrine. Beatrix has hot coffee waiting but the men make their own sandwiches.

Work starts by 5 am and continues until 8 am. This morning two-thirds of the crew are dredging silt for the first part of their shift while the rest push the filled wheelbarrows away and dump the spoil. Piet is an experienced boss and knows he will get the best from his team by rotating their tasks. At 8 there is a half-hour breakfast period when the men eat their sandwiches and drink the hot coffee brought by Beatrix. The next break comes at noon, when the whole crew returns to the hut for the main meal of the day – potatoes and cabbage, dotted with bacon fat and hard-boiled eggs. There is time for a brief nap and then work resumes at 1.30. At 4 there is another break for coffee with bread, then the last section of the shift, which ends around 7.

Evenings mean a wash followed by bread and hot cereal. Tonight Jan and Willem must do their share of potato peeling for the next day. But the day after that is Sunday, and time for the weekly bath, church and some indulgence in the spirit gin.

MAN AND WATER POWER   A Belgian painting of 1890 demonstrates how, on water, a single man could haul a cargo that weighed a few tons.

MOMENT OF TENSION A painting by the Belgian artist Constantin Meunier shows men removing a broken crucible at a glassworks. Each member of the team risks serious injury, and relies on the skill and effort of his fellows.

predictable consequences, as a witness told a committee of enquiry in 1842: 'Of minor accidents, burns are the most frequent. The upsetting or bursting of the bucket in which the melted metal is conveyed from the furnace to the casting place is the most common cause of these injuries. . . .' In 1906, Lady Bell, wife of a Middlesbrough ironmaster, assured her readers: 'Happily, serious accidents are comparatively rare' – and then noted that over the previous three years: 'One man had had his legs scalded from hot steam escaping from a boiler; another had his finger crushed by a piece of iron falling on it; eyes had been injured by explosions; [and] . . . one man had his foot crushed by a loaded barrow falling on it; one twisted his thigh by slipping while he was charging the furnace.'

In the worst accident of all at Middlesbrough two men, bowled over by a chance explosion, fell into a furnace of molten metal, charged to 1650°C (3000°F). It took two hours to recover what was left of them – and then work went on: 'In mines and coal-pits, after such an accident, nothing more is done during the day, and the mine or pit is laid idle. But at the ironworks the work cannot be interrupted; the furnaces cannot be allowed to go out; the regular succession of all that is done cannot be stopped; and the men who have seen the catastrophe which has overwhelmed their comrade go back, sick at heart, to continue their own work.'

FACTORIES AND FAMILIES

'Their labour is cheaper and they are more easily induced to undergo severe bodily fatigue than men, either for the praiseworthy motive of gaining additional support for their families, or from the folly of satisfying a love of dress': this is how a British factory inspector in the 1830s explained the textile industry's recruitment mostly of female workers. As the hours and conditions of children's employment were regulated, so female labour came increasingly to replace it. By 1839 there were nearly 300 000 cotton mill hands in Britain, of whom more than six out of ten were women. In woollen, silk and flax mills, where female dexterity surpassed that of the men in dealing with the troublesome fibres, the proportion was even higher.

At least one in four of the female workers was married, and contemporaries became alarmed at the implications of factory work for family life. Rather than caring for their infants in the home, many women had them brought to the factory three times during their shift to be suckled, either during their brief breaks at breakfast time and mid-day, or even while they continued working. Others farmed them out to home-working neighbours, such as laundresses, who dosed them liberally with 'Godfrey's Mixture', an opium-based sedative, to enable them to get on with their day's labour.

Another concern was the impact of factory employment on standards of housewifery. The girl who went into the mills as a child had little opportunity to learn from her mother the essential skills of cooking and sewing. In any case, as a working adult she would have no time to employ them, except in the evening, when she was exhausted, or on Sunday, when she ought to be in church. Furthermore, unmarried girls were thought to be at risk of sexual temptation in the mill.

Finally there was the threat to the authority of the head of the household. Since the husband and father was no longer the leader of a family production unit, he lost day-to-day supervision of his offspring, who were less inclined to give him unquestioning obedience. Worse still, it was possible to imagine a situation in which the man might be

A MILL GIRL IN MANCHESTER IN THE 1840S

IN 1842, the British factory re-former William Dodd published *The Factory System Illustrated* which included an account of the daily round of a typical teenage mill-hand. Too poor to own a clock, her family pays a watchman to tap on their window at 4.30 each morning. After dressing, the girl sips cold coffee and eats bread in the darkness and wraps her breakfast in a handkerchief. The clanging of the bell at the mill warns her of the need to hurry. The journey is a five-minute scamper in clumsy clogs over cobblestones slippery from the drizzle that makes Lancashire ideal for cotton spinning.

At 5.30, the day's work begins. Two hours later, the engines slacken. This allows the girl to clean her machines of dust and lint while they are still moving. If she is quick there is a little time for her to gobble the contents of her handkerchief. At noon, she cleans the machines more thoroughly before dashing home for soup and bread. Carrying a can of cold tea to drink through the afternoon shift, she is back in her place by 1 and works until 7. Then, after cleaning her machines yet again, she returns home some 14 hours after she first left it.

ARTIFICE, NOT ART
A woman and young girl assistant operate a silk-embroidering machine to imitate an expensive hand-woven original piece.

'This is repeated six days in the week (save that on Saturdays she may get back a little earlier) . . . This young woman looks very pale and delicate, and has every appear-ance of an approaching decline. I was asked to guess her age: I said, perhaps 15 . . . Her mother . . . told me she was going 19.'

---

unemployed and at home, while his wife and daughters were working at the mill, thus making him dependent on them, rather than vice versa – a total reversal of the 'natural' order of society.

These fears of mostly middle-class observers were often exaggerated. Even so, there was some truth in the arguments of people such as the British doctor Peter Gaskell who contended that in manufacturing districts the family was in a state of

crisis. It was a crisis whose causes 'have been wholly misunderstood. It is not poverty . . . no, it has arisen from the separation of families, the breaking up of households'. Many families tried to resist this trend, not least the handloom weavers, who worked ever longer hours to try to outpace the powerlooms. And in many cotton mills, family units did survive into the 1820s, with the spinner hiring and supervising his wife and two or three of his children as assistants. But then came larger machines, with so many spindles that each spinner needed up to nine assistants. Few men had that many offspring of working age and many were forced to hire other men's children.

SHOEMAKING SABOTEURS

The 'sabots', or wooden clogs, worn by French peasants were often poorly made and uncom-fortable to wear, with the result that cobblers who made leather boots of bad workmanship, and later any craftsmen guilty of such shoddiness, became known as 'saboteurs'. With the coming of the factories, the deliberate destruction of machinery by throwing a clog into its works – sabotage – became an obvious tactic in times of confrontation between workers and employers.

'STITCH, STITCH, STITCH'
With fingers weary and worn,
With eyelids heavy and red,
A woman sat, in unwomanly rags,
Plying her needle and thread.

The London poet Thomas Hood first published 'The Song of the Shirt' – a model for many later poems of social protest – in 1843. In it, he spotlighted one of the most important areas of female employment. The census of 1851, for example, reveals that Britain still had far more women earning their living with a needle (340 000) than by tending cotton machinery (272 000). A quarter of a century later, Paris had more seamstresses (51 169) than the city of Lyons had workers in all its silk mills (50 635).

Indeed, the French capital had a further 80 000 females employed in 21 other branches of the clothing trades alone. The most numerous were the 20 579 makers of shirts and linen, of whom the best paid were the embroiderers, especially those working in silver and gold. More than 7400 were employed in making artificial flowers, and a correspondent of the *New York Evening Post* wrote of France that 'a *fleuriste* can live very comfortably,

PIN MONEY A cartoon of 1849 in the magazine *Punch* denounces the exploitation of hand-seamstresses who earned pennies for working far into the night.

if she is not seized with a desire to deck her own person with the wreaths she makes'. Rolling cigars also paid women well, as did the jewellery trade. The same newspaper informed its readers that other specialised female occupations in France included ruby-cutting in the villages of the Jura mountains and braiding straw into hats at Nancy. Want of education limited a woman's entry into trades such as printing, and want of apprenticeship

GIRL AND MACHINE Thousands of young girls were still employed in US textile mills at the beginning of the 20th century. Protective legislation was hampered by the insistence of each state on passing its own.

WORK AND WORRIES
Women and children
clutch their loaves as free
bread is distributed to
needy villagers in a Belgian
painting of 1892 (above).
A French engraving of
a silk-reeling mill (right)
is another reminder that
working-class lives
remained dominated by
hard toil and the basic
struggle for survival.

forced her into low-skill
crafts such as making baskets, brooms, mats or
dusters. One of the most exploitative trades was toy-
making, geared entirely to the Christmas season:
'In November and December there are not enough
women to dress the dolls and ornament the
bonbons. Those who work have to sit up all night
and strain every nerve. To this activity succeed,
without the slightest transition, long months of
forced idleness.'

The general conclusion of the *New York Evening
Post* investigation into female labour conditions in
France was that: 'In general, talent only is well
paid. Persons who are endowed neither with talent
nor physical strength, can find profitable employment nowhere but in factories.' This often
involved work which was either dangerous or
disgusting. Glass-cutting was singled out as a

specific example: 'The business of cutting is generally entrusted to women in the factories. They do
it marvelously well, as it requires only patience and
skill. Unfortunately, it is a very unhealthy trade, as
the necessity of bending over the wheel and having
their hands in water all day, exposes them to
dangerous pulmonary infections.'

Flax-spinning was also considered particularly
unpleasant: 'Preparations of hemp and flax . . . emit
. . . quantities of very unwholesome dust. It is
impossible to card and spin them, except in very
hot rooms, and with the aid of abundance of water.
Few sights are more unpleasant . . . The water
floods the brick floors and the smell of the flax in
the heated atmosphere produces an intolerable
stench. The greater part of the workwomen are
obliged to lay aside most of their clothes, are

EYEWITNESS

FINEABLE OFFENCES AT A MANCHESTER COTTON MILL: 1823

Any spinner found with his window open . . . 1 shilling
Any spinner found dirty at his work . . . 1 shilling
Any spinner found washing himself . . . 1 shilling
Any spinner heard whistling . . . 1 shilling
Any spinner found putting his gas out too soon . . .
   1 shilling

Any spinner spinning with gaslight too long in the
   morning . . . 2 shillings
Any spinner being five minutes late after the last bell
   rings . . . 1 shilling
Any spinner being sick and cannot find another
   spinner to give satisfaction . . . 6 shillings

crowded together in this pestilent atmosphere, and stand all day long perspiring, and with naked feet, the water often reaching their ankles. When, after 12 hours' hard work, they leave the factory for their homes, the wraps with which they cover themselves barely afford an adequate protection against the cold and damp.'

The most typical French female factory worker, however, was a silk-worker in Lyons. The survey calculated that: 'To be miserably lodged, clothed and fed and, with all this to be obliged to work, at the very least, 12 hours a day, is the fate of a female weaver, as favourably situated as possible.' For an American readership such revelations were doubly shocking, for the United States had pioneered a very different kind of industrial order.

An Industrial Idyll

In 1813 Francis Cabot Lowell, bearer of the names of two distinguished New England dynasties, established the Boston Manufacturing Company with a capital of $500 000. Its factory at Waltham, Massachusetts, became North America's first integrated textile factory, processing cotton from bale to spindle to loom, all under one roof. Less than a decade later, the company established an even more ambitious enterprise on the Merrimack river at Chelmsford in the same state. Within three years, the population rose from 300 to 2000 and the community, acknowledging the source of its expansion, renamed itself Lowell.

Within five years, Lowell had become an industrial showpiece and an essential stop on the itinerary of the note-taking tourist. In 1828 an English visitor recorded his astonishment at the sight at 6 am of a town 'speckled over with girls . . . glittering with bright shawls and showy-coloured gowns, all streaming along . . . with . . . an elasticity of step implying an obvious desire to get to their work'. Fourteen years later, the English novelist Charles Dickens was similarly surprised by this army of well-dressed, healthy industrial workers with 'the manners and deportment of young women, not of degraded brutes'. The contrast with Lancashire mill-girls could not have been more striking. It was, in Dickens' words, the difference 'between Good and Evil, the living light and deepest shadow'.

The 'Lowell girl' became a distinct social type. Often the daughter of a substantial farmer, storekeeper or craftsman, she had a good opinion of her own worth and a clear aim – to leave the mill within a few years with a 'bottom drawer', or nest-egg of $300 to $400. Some helped to pay off their family's mortgage or to send younger brothers through college. Others put themselves through college, working alternate years at the mill, until they graduated and could become teachers.

The Lowell girls worked a 12 hour day in summer and from sunrise to sunset in winter, but they were well paid and, once half their wages had gone for room and board, they had cash to spare. They lived in boarding houses that were approved and inspected by the company and could be struck off for failing to maintain the expected standards of cleanliness and morality. Girls slept two or four to a room, rather than in dormitories, and cultivated colourful windowboxes. On Sundays attendance

Surprise Offering
A magazine produced by girls employed in the Lowell mills in Massachusetts was a rare example of culture from, rather than for, the masses.

37

COSTUME DRAMA An exquisite 18th-century kimono (top) combines hand-embroidery with stencilling. In a European-style silk-reeling factory in Japan (above), only the male supervisors wear Western dress. Women, meanwhile, peel vegetables and dry dishes in a traditional Japanese kitchen (right) that remains innocent of imported manufactures.

at church was compulsory, while 'ardent spirits' (alcohol) and 'games of hazard or cards' were forbidden; the girls were, however, encouraged to subscribe to newspapers and lending libraries, and to organise sewing circles, improving lectures and even a literary periodical *The Lowell Offering*.

It was too good to last and it didn't. In 1834 and 1836, wage cuts were met with 'indignation meetings' and strikes. The strike leaders were blacklisted; and a much tougher regime introduced, with workers recruited from the Irish and the French Canadians. The girls whom one observer had described as 'fair, unveil'd Nuns of Industry, Sisters of Thrift' had vanished.

An Industrial Empire: The Cockerills of Seraing

THE FIRST mainland European country to follow Britain on the path of industrialisation was Belgium. Here William Cockerill (1759-1832), a Lancashire blacksmith who remained illiterate to the end of his days, built the first wool-carding and wool-spinning machines on the Continent.

In 1807 he established a factory for making textile machinery at Seraing, near Liège. By 1819, under the direction of his son, John, the Seraing works employed 3000 men, organised in seven departments, each headed by an Englishman. It also had its own coal mine and iron foundry. It was soon exporting machinery and engines to France, Germany, Spain, Italy and Russia, and it supplied all the early locomotives on the Belgian and Prussian railways.

By 1872, the Seraing works had four collieries, five blast furnaces, two foundries, ten Bessemer converters for making steel, 254 engines and brickworks turning out 15 million bricks a year. There were 8912 employees, including 420 who ran its internal railway system. The company also had its own shipyard at Antwerp and mines that guaranteed its supply of iron for 100 years ahead. Company welfare provision included a free dispensary, a hospital, an orphanage and a pension scheme.

HERO OR VICTIM? An exhausted 'puddler' at the Seraing works was the inspiration for Constantin Meunier's painting *Weariness*.

Half a century later Japan, too, produced its own – very different – female mill-workers. Desperate to earn foreign exchange, the modernising government focused on the silk industry. In 1870, the first silk-reeling spinning factory was opened under the direction of a Swiss expert, and in 1872 the government, with French technical assistance, opened its own model plant at Tomioka.

Silk Splashed with Tears

Within a decade most of the workers were girls from impoverished families. Their fathers, often illiterate, signed contracts which virtually condemned them to bonded slavery for five or seven years. The family received advances against the girl's wages that could be used to pay off debts or rent. Some contracts specified that the girls would be paid nothing for their first year on the grounds that they were learning their trade. One even stipulated that if the girl quit not only would she have to return the 5 Yen advance paid to her father but also forfeit all her earnings to date and pay a 50 Yen fine to compensate her employer for his inconvenience.

As late as 1893, when Japan was producing almost a quarter of the world's raw silk, Japanese mill-girls were paid one-tenth of the wages of their British counterparts. Girls in the cotton industry were paid less even than their counterparts in Indian mills, and they faced the extra hazard of inhaling cotton lint, which led to a high incidence of tuberculosis. The pace of work was unrelenting, as one mill-girl later recalled: 'From morning, while it was still dark, we worked in the lamplit factory till ten at night . . . When we worked late into the night, they occasionally gave us a yam. We then had to do our washing, fix our hair and so on. By then it would be 11 o'clock. There was no heat even in the winter, and so we had to sleep huddled together. Several of the girls ran back [home] . . . If we didn't do the job right we were scolded, and, if we did better than others, the others resented it. The life of a woman is really awful.'

The best girls could return to their families for the annual festival with 100 Yen – more than many farmers could earn in the same period and enough to build a two-storey house. Hard as factory work was, many girls preferred it to the backbreaking labour of the dung-laden rice paddies. Silk-reeling was dry, indoor work and most girls also ate better than they did at home, where they ranked bottom in the hierarchy of the family. Some even enjoyed the occasional luxury of a hot bath. And many thought it better than being sold into the uncertain opportunities offered by a geisha house.

THE WORLD OF THE COALMINER

Coal was basic to the Industrial Revolution. It was the source of energy for all

steam-based technology in both industry and transport. It was also a vital ingredient

in the production of metals, chemicals and gas.

THE preindustrial world relied on wood for many of its needs. It was the raw material for buildings, for ships, for furniture, for carts and for countless other items of daily use, as well as the fuel for industry and the home. But this intensive use of wood meant that in many regions and countries it came to be in short supply – as early as the 16th century in the case of south-east England. 'Sea-coal', transported to London on ships from the north-east of the country was the first solution to the English fuel crisis. Later, coal would be the power behind the Industrial Revolution, providing fuel for steam engines and, after that, for locomotives; it was also essential in the smelting of iron and the production of gas.

All across Europe and North America, coal made industrialisation possible by providing what seemed to be a limitless reservoir of energy. By 1800 Britain,

IN THE COUNTRY An English painting of around 1820 emphasises the rural setting of many coal mines. The pithead equipment includes steam-powered winding gear and a machine for weighing laden carts.

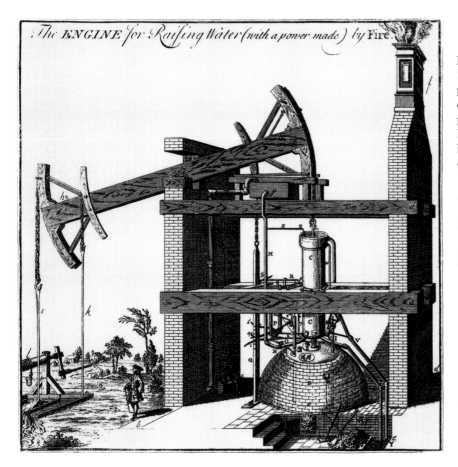

The ENGINE for Raising Water (with a power made) by Fire.

PIONEER An engraving of 1717 is the earliest known picture of a 'Newcomen' colliery pumping engine, probably at Coventry in the English Midlands. The human figure indicates its enormous size.

which led the way in exploiting coal as in most areas of industry, was using over 10 million tons of it a year. To produce the energy equivalent in human muscle power would have required a food supply sufficient to nourish 85 million adult males – at a time when Britain's population was little more than a tenth of that figure. As G.R. Porter's mid-century *Progress of the Nation* noted exultantly, Britain's coal mines were 'the source of greater riches than ever issued from the mines of Peru'.

Until the end of the 17th century, it was seldom possible to work mines of any kind at depths of more than a few score yards beneath the surface; deeper than that problems of flooding and ventilation became insuperable. At the same time, mining leases often ignored rights over seams deeper than 60 fathoms (360 ft – 110 m) in the conviction that they were unworkable. Celia Fiennes, visiting Cornish tin mines in the 1690s, noted with surprise

that men were employed even on the Lord's Day to keep the workings from flooding. One colliery in Warwickshire was obliged to employ 500 horses to hoist out water, bucket by bucket, at a cost in feed alone of £900 per year. Despite these limitations, however, in 1700 there were already some 60 pits around Tyneside in the north-east, producing a million tons of coal a year.

The invention of a simple pump-action 'beam-engine' by Thomas Savery, and its improvement by Thomas Newcomen, enabled miners to work at far greater depths, however. Not only did it pump out water but, by the end of the 18th century, it was regularly used to haul up the coal as well. By 1778 there were at least 137 Newcomen engines at work in the coalfields of Tyne and Wear. Five collieries had four engines each, another had five and one had six. Writing in the same decade, the Scottish economist and philosopher Adam Smith estimated that no less than a third of all British shipping was employed in hauling coal from Newcastle to London – from where it was taken as far as Oxford by river. This great 'nursery of sailors' was a vital reserve for the Royal Navy in time of war.

The much more efficient Boulton and Watt

ONE-WAY HAULAGE A boy operates the brake on a Newcastle coal wagon as it descends by gravity to a 'staithe' for unloading. The horse will haul the empty wagon back up the tramway.

SUPERSTITIONS AND SAFETY IN THE DURHAM COALFIELD

A REPORTER for the British *Morning Chronicle* informs his readers of superstitions that were current in the Durham coalfields in the 1840s: ❝ . . . the mining population, particularly the hewers, are still very attentive to signs and omens before they commence their day's work. They account it specially unlucky to cross a woman on their way to the pit . . . many a miner, if he catches a glimpse . . . of the flutter of a female dress, will turn on his heel and go back to bed again. A gentleman informed me that he had once unwittingly stopped the day's working of a pit by passing, when the men were going to their labour, wrapped up in a light-coloured plaid. He afterwards learned that there was a grand consultation held . . . and that it was unanimously resolved that nothing could be more rash than going into the pit after several of the party had distinctly seen a ghost. ❞

engines, first installed in the north-east in 1778, enabled sinkings to go even deeper – 600 ft (180 m) by 1802, 840 ft (255 m) by 1810 and 1800 ft (550 m) by 1830. By 1829 there were 21 000 men working in the Tyne and Wear collieries many of which employed more than 300 men, and an even larger number involved in handling and transporting the coal. The Cumbrian coalfield, though smaller, was technically no less advanced. By 1813 the Lowther family's mines employed 600 men and 1000 horses, had 20 miles (32 km) of underground railroads and were also linked to an ironworks.

In that same year, however, a visitor to the port of Whitehaven, from which coal was exported, mainly to Ireland, recoiled with disgust at the very sight of the local labour force, and especially the 'girls . . . ragged and beastly in their appearance, and with a shameless indecency in their behaviour . . . All the people whom we met with were distinguished by an extraordinary wretchedness; immoderate labour and a noxious atmosphere had marked their countenances with signs of disease and decay; they were mostly half-naked, blackened all over with dirt, and altogether so miserably disfigured and abused, that they looked like a race fallen from the common rank of men and doomed, as in a kind of purgatory, to wear away their lives in these dismal shades'.

CLEAN COAL IN PENNSYLVANIA

In 1698 a Welsh immigrant to Pennsylvania had noted that 'the runs of water have the same colour as that which proceeds from the Coal Mines in Wales'. But wood was so cheap and plentiful, both there and in Virginia, that coalmining opportunities were largely neglected, until the Revolutionary War interrupted the imports from England and Nova Scotia on which a number of industrial users had come to rely.

By 1800, however, Pittsburgh's smoky skies were already provoking local disquiet, though New York and New England were to prove more fortunate, thanks to clean-burning anthracite from eastern Pennsylvania. The legendary cleanness of this fuel gave birth to the myth of a ghostly figure who rode the line, remembered in a contemporary rhyme:

When Phoebe Snow sets out to go
From New York City to Buffalo,
She travels white,
Arrives clean and bright
On the Road of Anthracite.

Her laundry bill for fluff and frill
Miss Phoebe finds is nearly nil.
It's always light, though gowns of white
Are worn on the Road of Anthracite.

After Britain, the most advanced coal industry in Europe was that of Belgium, notably around Liège. Around 1840, the French, too, began to exploit their coal reserves intensively, although a British visitor was staggered to see pits over 1800 ft (550 m) deep where face-workers were still required to reach their work stations entirely by ladders.

From the speculator's point of view, mining remained a risky business. There were just so many imponderables – geology, technology, finance, demand and, not least, the labour force. In 1809 the Arigna venture, employing 253 men in Connaught, Ireland, was estimated to have lost its backers £60 000. One observer, reporting on Lord Wandesford's Leinster collieries in 1844, blamed a weak management structure: 'As the working was carried on without any rule by every small tenant, not only a great deal of valuable coal was lost . . . but another large proportion stolen, or sold by the master colliers, who had the workings in their respective hands without accounting.'

Relying on physical strength for their earning power, miners achieved their peak incomes relatively young, a factor which encouraged early marriage and hence large families. Earnings could be high but were unreliable. Apart from lost time

BLIND ALLEY   German miners of around 1900 display their safety lamps. Although some miners went for months in winter without seeing full daylight, many horses never surfaced at all and went blind.

caused by engine breakdowns or cave-ins, there was invariably a fall in demand for home-heating coal each summer. Earning power was also clearly related to status. Surface workers ranked lower than underground workers. But even they had a hierarchy of their own – ranging from skilled carpenters, farriers and boilermakers down to unskilled labourers who sorted and stacked pit props, and women, boys and the disabled who picked out stones that had been mined during each shift. At the apex of this surface hierarchy stood the man in charge of the engine driving the cage that took the miners to and from the coalface. Twice a day he held the lives of hundreds of men in his hands.

Underground, half the men were employed in

transporting the coal from the working seams up to the surface. The rest were 'getters', the elite of the underground workers, who knelt or lay on their sides to hack out the coal with a pick: the scars and callouses on their elbows and backs were badges of honour.

Past the age of 40, few faceworkers could expect to keep up with their younger mates. A tiny minority of the literate, sober and responsible might look forward to promotion to a supervisory or safety job, but for most, age relegated them to the surface, where they had started as boys, a cycle illustrated in a British folk song:

> *Oh, my name is Geordie Black, I'm getting very old,*
> *I've hewed tons of coal in my time,*
> *And when I was young I could either put or hew,*
> *Out of other lads I always took the shine.*
> *I'm gannin down the hill, I cannot use the pick.*
> *The master has no pity on old bones.*
> *I'm noo on the bank, I pass my time away,*
> *Among the bits of lads with picking out the stones.*

DIET, EARNINGS AND HEALTH

Heavy labour required a heavy diet. The budget of a Durham miner around 1790 reveals the major items of annual expenditure as barley (150s a year) and oatmeal (104s), followed by wheat and rye (50s), butter and meat (50s each), tea and sugar (40s), milk (30s) and potatoes (28s). Candles and soap accounted for a further 30s, and hard wear and tear probably explained the surprisingly high annual expenditure of 100s on boots and clothes.

A solid diet might sustain a miner's stamina, and thus his earning power, but there was much to undermine it. The most obvious was bad air; a foul mine could send the strongest man into a swoon or have him hastily returned to the daylight, coughing uncontrollably. The atmosphere was not improved by the complete absence of sanitary arrangements. Miners relieved themselves where they could.

Improvements in underground ventilation proved a mixed blessing, for 19th-century miners worked far longer shifts than their grandfathers had. The constant damp caused ague. The cramped working postures led to muscular complaints. And extremes of hot and cold caused fevers. Measurements taken at a Jarrow colliery in the English north-east in 1820 showed a temperature at the surface of 8°C (46°F); at the pit bottom, 810 ft (245 m) below, it was 16°C (61°F); in the worst-ventilated part of the workings 24°C (75°F); and in the boiler room an insupportable 62°C (144°F).

Furthermore, there was the possibility on every shift of sudden death or permanent invalidity resulting from a rock-fall or explosion caused by an accumulation of natural gases or faulty explosives. Between 1850 and 1914 the average fatality rate in the British mining industry was around 100 a year. Of these, teenagers – impetuous but often fatally ignorant of the risks they ran – were twice as likely to die as adults. And for every fatal injury, the records of miners' benevolent funds reveal numerous non-fatal accidents – each leading to an average of 30 days off work. This meant that at least one-sixth of Britain's mining labour force was seriously injured every single working year. Moreover, three out of every four who died did so as a result, not of the horrific explosions or cave-ins that made

MODEL WORKER Many artists – such as the Belgian Constantin Meunier here – idealised the miner as the archetype of working-class dignity. In fact, most were small and wiry men.

TOPSIDE Surface work in mines was often as arduous as underground labour, but worse paid. Workers might be relegated to working 'topside' if too badly injured or weak to continue working underground.

the national headlines, but from the unspectacular daily accidents which were accepted as inevitable. As late as the 1930s, the writer George Orwell noted how miners saw nothing remarkable in the weekly purchase of a 'death stamp' to furnish emergency funds for the unexpectedly bereaved.

Most pervasive of all dangers was dust, which caused bronchitis, asthma, the lung disease silicosis and nystagmus, an eye complaint that left the pupils perpetually rolling in the head, and incapable of correct focus. Finally, like other labourers, a miner was vulnerable to the strains involved in routine heavy lifting.

In Russia, miners often lived in all-male 'housing' provided by the mining company in conditions which could actually aggravate rather than relieve the damage done to them by their work, as the report of a local government inspector in the Donbass industrial region in the 1880s makes

EYEWITNESS

'DEAR MARGARET': A MINER'S FAREWELL TO HIS WIFE

These touching words were found scratched on a water bottle belonging to Michael Smith, one of 164 miners who died trapped in the pit after an explosion at Seaham colliery in 1880.

❛ Dear Margaret there was forty alltogether at 7 a.m. Some were singing Hymns but my thoughts were on my little Michael that him and I would meet in heaven at the same time. Oh Dear Wife, God save you and the children and pray for me. Dear Wife Farewell, my last thoughts are about you and the children, be shure and learn the children to pray for me. Oh what an awfull position we are in. ❜

clear: 'The floor is earth and there is no ceiling – instead there is a roof of earth on rafters. Inside is a cooking stove, a chair and a bench to sit on; beds are exceptional. Dampness and moisture come through the roof and walls and consequently the air in the dwelling is constantly stuffy and mouldy even in summer. Tiny windows with dirty glass allow dim half-light to enter the dwelling. In this way the workers, suffocating in the stifling and heavy atmosphere of the underground galleries, during their day and night work, and ruining their eyesight under the dim flicker of a smoky oil lamp, are deprived of sufficient light and clean fresh air even during their rest. Thanks to all this the collier is an emaciated, understrength figure with a sickly pale colour to his face and bad eyesight. . . .

'The same mines . . . are maintained defectively; cave-ins frequently occur, because of which the already inadequate ventilation of underground passages becomes even worse and the air in the passages thickens to the point that the lamps go out. . . .'

RECRUITMENT, DISCIPLINE AND EXPLOITATION

Many collieries had trouble recruiting a workforce. They were often situated in isolated rural areas and their workers – by the nature of the job separated from any neighbours during the long working hours – were often regarded locally with fear, suspicion or disdain. Isolation – social as well as physical – resulted in generations of miners following one another down the pit. In the coalfields of northern France, company policies often gave such traditions a nudge. Housing was provided to attract new workers and to retain those who had

LAYERS OF LABOUR   Top: Hand-operated winding-gear at a shallow mine. Middle: 'Putters' hauling underground. Bottom: Naked 'getters' crouching and prone.

key skills. Families that produced boys were often 'promoted' to better housing, from two rooms to three; this gave the parents more privacy in which to produce more, hopefully male, offspring.

Attracting additional hands in times of rapid expansion could be especially difficult. Frequently men were drawn from far away, where prospects might be grim enough to make even mining look attractive. Thus the South Wales coalfields were populated by men whose ancestors' bones lay beside repossessed smallholdings in Ireland or worked-out copper-mines in Cornwall. Between 1841 and 1901 Britain's colliery districts attracted no fewer than 500 000 migrants from rural areas.

Recruitment difficulties, and the need to lure the next generation down the pit as soon as possible, partly explain the horrific findings of Britain's 1840 Children's Employment Commission: that eight or nine was the regular starting age for work, though boys as young as four were recorded down the mines; that 'trappers', operating ventilation doors, worked quite alone in total darkness, for an average of 12 hours per shift; and, most shocking of all to the Victorian mind, that 'the girls and boys, and the young men and young women, and even married women and women with child, commonly work almost naked, and the men, in many mines, quite naked; and that all classes of witnesses bear testimony to the demoralising influence of the employment of females underground'. As a result, in 1842 the British Parliament forbade the employment underground of boys younger than ten and females of any age whatsoever.

Making men come to work was another problem.

THE MOLLY MAGUIRES: A NOT-SO-SECRET SOCIETY

IN THE 1840s, an Irish widow called Molly Maguire led a protest movement against her country's landlords. When a secret society of miners was accused of acts of terrorism in the anthracite fields of eastern Pennsylvania and West Virginia in the 1870s, they were named after her.

Outrage among the miners had been provoked by low pay, appalling working conditions, exploitation at company stores and blatant anti-Catholic discrimination in hiring practices. They responded with arson and explosions, intimidation and assassination. The mine owners became convinced that an Irish welfare and social club, the Ancient Order of Hibernians, was being used as a front by the 'Mollies'. Led by Franklin B.

LADIES IN WAITING Pennsylvania miners' wives made their homes in flimsy shacks and stuck by their men through bloody confrontations.

Gowen, President of the Philadelphia Coal and Iron Company, they hired James McParlan, a Pinkerton detective, to infiltrate the group. A series of sensational trials between 1875 and 1877 hinged on McParlan's testimony and led to the conviction and then hanging of ten alleged 'Mollies' in June 1877.

A month later the US experienced further unrest in its first national strike when workers on the Baltimore and Ohio Railroad protested against a second wage-cut in four years. In the accompanying violence nine strikers were shot dead in Baltimore and 19 in Chicago; a Pittsburgh mob put 2000 railroad cars to the torch.

In 1859 one French coalmine was fining its men a day and a half's wages for a day's absenteeism. In 1862 it changed tack, offering bonuses for regular attendance, and in 1867 it changed the system once again by offering the bonuses to shift foremen, rather than to the men themselves. This did not last long. In 1868 the fines were raised to two and a half days' pay. The problem of attendance was not really solved until a widespread depression led to substantial layoffs and the opportunity for management to change the entire structure of shift-working hours in 1871. Men desperately anxious to hold on to their jobs, could scarcely spare a thought, let alone time, for their smallholdings – the chief cause of absenteeism in that particular area.

Attendance does not guarantee performance. Many managements favoured a piece-work system on the grounds

OVERSHADOWED Immigrant children in this anthracite-mining community in eastern Pennsylvania had little chance of education and so most remained tied to the pits.

SAFETY WITH THE DAVY LAMP

IN 1815 the British Society for Preventing Accidents in Coal Mines commissioned the scientist Humphry Davy to investigate conditions under which firedamp (methane) and air mix and explode. Davy was the foremost experimental scientist of his day, and had been knighted in England and given one of France's top awards – even though the countries were at war. The result of his researches was a safety lamp shielding the naked flame with a double layer of metal gauze; it would remain standard miners' equipment until the advent of electric lighting in the 20th century.

In gratitude some English mine owners presented Davy with a handsome service of plate. Their gratitude was probably motivated by the prospect of more profits. The Davy lamp allowed them to exploit deep but extensive coal reserves previously regarded as unworkably dangerous. Miners continued, however, an earlier custom of taking caged canaries with them. These warned them of gases that caused suffocation – a suffocated canary was a signal to clear out.

LIFESAVER Sir Humphry Davy's 'safety lamp' gained him worldwide renown.

DEEP MINING Safety lamps enabled miners, like this young American, to work deeper and narrower seams than ever before.

---

that it generally raised output while diminishing the need for paid supervision. An alternative tack was to provide welfare benefits, with the aim of weakening trade unionism, stabilising the labour force and allowing management to accuse recalcitrant workers of 'ingratitude'. Employers often donated land and materials for the construction of churches or chapels, while miners provided the labour. Libraries and reading rooms were also provided, where men could read books and newspapers, and attend first-aid classes and lectures on mine safety and the value of temperance.

In France, Belgium and Britain, miners often responded to acts of paternalism by establishing their own, self-financed and self-governed institutions, beyond the manipulation of the employers or churches. These included social security schemes and shops, run on cooperative lines, which freed miners from reliance on company shops and were often managed by trade unionists who had been dismissed for agitation and black-listed from further employment in mining.

Drinking was central to the life of most miners. In England, a Shropshire vicar in 1800 denounced local colliers for turning their 'enormous bellies into moving hogsheads', and temptation was hard to avoid. The Durham mining village of Hetton-le-Hole, for example, had one public house for every 33 inhabitants. Agents advertising pubs for sale often noted the proximity of a mine or foundry as a virtual guarantee of its profitability. Apart from pubs, there were also beer shops, licensed grocers, eating houses and semi-secret 'clubs' run on a 'non-profit' principle.

However, drinking was more than an indulgence or a path to oblivion. Until the mid-19th century, tea and coffee were expensive, and milk and water suspect on health grounds. Strong drink, on the other hand, was associated with vigour and manliness and especially welcome to a dry throat at the end of a dust-laden day. The fact that weekly wages were often paid out in a pub made an evening of heavy drinking an almost unavoidable ritual to mark the end of a working week.

STRIKE!

The dangers of a miner's life, the premium placed on toughness and the solidarity between miners, combined with the immense gulf in wealth and lifestyle between the collier and the coalowner to impart a special bitterness to mining disputes. When the coalowners of Durham altered the timing of 'binding' to the miners' disadvantage in the winter of 1809-10, the men came out on strike in protest. Custom decreed that the 'binding' of men to their annual contract should be in October, and from the miners' point of view this date had much to commend it. It enabled them to take advantage of the pre-Christmas peak demand for coal to force up the bounty paid for signing on. The owners countered with the offer of a four-month contract, renewable in January. So many 'ringleaders' were arrested in the course of the ensuing dispute that Durham jail was filled, the House of Correction was filled, and the bishop's stables pressed into service to take yet more. In all 159 men were imprisoned.

In the same coalfield a pitmen's strike in 1832, and an employers' lockout in 1844, were accompanied by evictions from company housing. 'Paternalistic' employers did not scruple to build whole settlements without even a cesspool or, sometimes, a single privy. But forcible eviction from any home, however wretched, invariably caused a sense of violation and betrayal. In 1844 the victims were reduced to living in tents. It is hardly surprising, then, that blacklegs were regularly intercepted, beaten and stripped of their clothes which, with their tools, were then thrown down the pit shaft.

In Wales miners' unions stealthily established themselves under the cloak of the 'Friendly Society', the poor man's do-it-yourself social security system. Men who met regularly, paid subscriptions, and kept accounts and lists of membership, could always exclude 'strangers' willing to work for lower than the going rate.

DOORSTEP DELIVERY Coal became the universal domestic fuel in the industrial world and was distributed from depots, usually at railway stations.

A 56 day strike at the Anzin mines near Valenciennes in northern France in 1884 inspired one of Emile Zola's greatest novels, *Germinal.* Zola had already decided to write a novel about miners when the Anzin dispute erupted. Posing as the secretary of a sympathetic local member of parliament, he visited the area, interrogated the strikers and their wives, and went 2000 ft (610 m) underground to experience coal-face conditions for himself. In his search for authenticity, Zola also read extensively about the industrial diseases of miners and the techniques of mine engineering. He dedicated the first ten chapters of the novel to 24 hours in the life of a mining community: where a family of nine sleep in a single bedroom; where the streets are clogged with 'a mud peculiar to coalmining areas, black with soot in suspension, thick and so sticky that clogs came off in it '; and where the only public buildings are ugly brick churches, which look like furnaces, and beer shops in such profusion that 'for a thousand houses there were more than five hundred taverns'. Zola portrayed in minute detail the conditions which reduced the miner to the level of an animal 'crushed, underfed, ill-educated'.

Two decades after the publication of *Germinal* the French coalfields witnessed a disaster that might have defied even the pen of a Zola to portray. An underground gas explosion at Courrières in 1906 killed 1200 men. The disaster helped to trigger a strike by some 61 000 miners, protesting against the conditions that allowed such accidents to occur, and in Paris twice as many more workers joined in. During the two-month dispute, violence against the police and non-strikers made it a 'classic' miners' strike – a convulsion which commanded wide sympathy among working people but could not alter the fundamental insecurities that were part of the miner's way of life.

THE SURVIVAL OF THE ARTISAN

Artisans, often grounded in skills that had accumulated over centuries, were the people

who literally carried their livelihood in their hands. The Industrial Revolution

challenged their standing but paradoxically increased their numbers.

THE typical worker of the preindustrial world was an artisan who used simple tools to make sophisticated products, such as jewellery, furniture, lace or books. The archetypal worker of the industrial world, by contrast, was the factory operative, who used sophisticated machines to make simple products, such as cotton cloth, nails or knives and forks. However, the rise of the factory worker did not imply the fall of the artisan – indeed, the number of artisans increased throughout the first century of industrialisation. In the France of 1850, 1.3 million industrial workers were employed by firms with 11 or

more on their payroll, while more than 1.5 million were employed in firms of ten or less. In 1851 Britain, the world's most advanced industrial country, had twice as many building craftsmen as coalminers, twice as many tailors as ironworkers, twice as many blacksmiths as makers of machines and boilers, and twice as many lacemakers as shipbuilders.

Nevertheless, the new technologies and ways of working did force the artisan to adapt. People who had begun their working lives mastering the

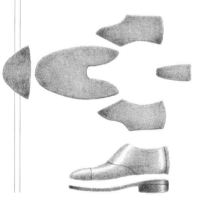

FOOTLOOSE A Dutch painting of 1630 (top) depicts an itinerant artisan cobbler. The sewing machine introduced mass production to shoemaking, as in a factory in Northampton, England, around 1900 (right). Workers, usually women, simply assembled ready-made parts (below).

COUNTRY CRAFTS **Rural craftsmen in Japan use indigo to dye stencilled patterns on cloth. Many country-dwellers combined farming with off-season handwork.**

techniques required to make an entire product from start to finish might end it repetitively toiling away at a single stage, process or subcomponent. Rather than submit to that fate, a European craftsman might emigrate to one of his country's colonies where skills of every sort were in demand.

MOBILITY AND IMMOBILITY

Traditionally, artisans had been distinguished from other workers by their skill (usually acquired through seven-year apprenticeships), by possessing a modest capital in tools, materials and stock, by their literacy and by their capacity for organisation in defence of their trade. Typically, they defended themselves through the guild, which combined the functions of technical college, insurance company, trading standards office and social club. The guilds provided the normal career structure from apprentice to journeyman to master. To enlarge his experience, a qualified young journeyman would tramp round the country, confident

that his credentials would secure him a welcome, a bed and refreshment at the least, and possibly a job as well in each place where his trade was practised.

Thomas Hodgskin, who toured north Germany around 1820, noted that young men, on completing their apprenticeship, were actually compelled to spend three years wandering from town to town before being allowed to settle or marry. Failure to comply with these requirements was punished by expulsion from the guild and thus a lifetime as an unskilled labourer. Hodgskin judged the system by the time he saw it to be little better than compulsory vagabondage.

Guilds withered away in England in the 18th century as their concern to enforce rigid standards over skills, prices and conditions of work came increasingly to be vilified as an unjustifiable restraint on trade. And in revolutionary France they were swept away by decree in 1791. In central and eastern Europe, however, guilds lingered longer into the 19th century, and in some areas their members made common cause with reactionary landowners against the disruptive impact of technological and commercial innovation. Numbers were also on their side. In relatively advanced Prussia,

THE ARTISAN AS IDEAL

Social critics such as the Englishmen William Morris and John

Ruskin idealised the self-sufficient virtues of the artisan.

THE HARD-NOSED, practical artisan who made up the mid-19th-century 'aristocracy of labour' was either a product of industrialisation, such as the engineer, or had proved wily and resilient enough to keep up with it, such as the printer. Such solid folk were a far cry from the moral heroes idealised by the British art critic John Ruskin (1819-1900) and his disciple William Morris (1834-96). Their legacy was an 'Arts and Crafts Movement' which was to prove immensely influential both in Britain and abroad.

Ruskin argued that European culture had taken a wrong turning at the Renaissance. By exalting the artist and 'fine art' as an end in itself, it had automatically denigrated the craftsman. Instead, he advocated a return to medieval creativity, when artist and craftsman had been one, and the weaving of a tapestry for use in the home had been no less an art than the carving of a statue to adorn a cathedral. William Morris devoted his prolific talents and volcanic energy to putting this doctrine into

practice. He tried painting, making furniture and designing stained glass before focusing his efforts on pattern designing and the manufacture of carpets, curtains, dress materials, tapestries and wallpapers. Even in his own lifetime, Morris had a deep impact on the taste and lifestyle of the European and American middle classes. Through the firm of Morris and Co, he supplied a range of well-made, durable and reasonably priced goods, from

REVOLUTIONARY TRADITIONALIST William Morris, aged 55, wears the rough clothes of a working man (right). The frontispiece of his futuristic fable, *News from Nowhere,* **depicts his country retreat, Kelmscott Manor.**

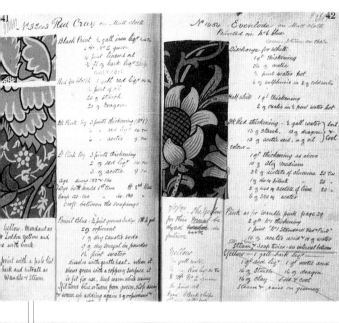

rush-bottomed 'Sussex' chairs for the drawing room to floral-patterned tiles for the kitchen and bathroom and bright bird-motif hangings for the bedroom.

Both Ruskin and Morris deplored the impact of mechanisation on the design and quality of household goods, believing that machine methods produced goods more cheaply but to lower standards. Both also believed that the subdivision of labour that accompanied mechanisation destroyed

BACK TO BASICS Morris kept records of his experiments with vegetable dyes (top left). His designs were based on natural forms, such as the pomegranate (above right). Employees (above left) knew that he could perform most tasks better than they could.

the satisfaction of true 'work', replacing it with meaningless, soul-sickening 'labour'.

Morris's ideas inspired the establishment of various 'Guilds' – a name self-consciously reminis-

cent of medieval craftsmanship – to provide honestly crafted goods for a discerning clientele. For example, the Century Guild, founded by the British architect A.H. Mackmurdo in 1882, followed the precedent of Morris & Co in manufacturing furniture, textiles and metalwork. The sinuous flame and flower motifs of many Century Guild designs were clear anticipations of the broader artistic movement that was to become known as Art Nouveau.

SWINDLES AT THE SWEATSHOP

AN ANONYMOUS informant describes conditions in the New York clothing trade around 1890:

❛ An ad in a Long Island paper called for a woman to sew on buttons. . . After making a satisfactory sample I was told the price was 2 cents for a gross; no thread supplied. Bewildered, I made some mental multiplication, but I could not think of more than 60 cents for 30 gross of buttons. Of this I subtracted 5 cents for cotton and 30 cents for car fare, which left a total of 25 cents earnings. However, I was elated at being of some help, and set to work as soon as I reached home. It took me one whole week to mount the 4320 buttons and when I delivered them . . . I was told that only ten gross were mounted properly; that all I could get was 30 cents and would I call next Saturday.

My next experience was neckties. I made four samples . . . which took from 9 o'clock in the morning until 3 o'clock in the afternoon. Then when the

HOMEWORK An 1889 photograph by social crusader Jacob Riis exposes the squalor of a New York tenement tailoring sweatshop.

fourth bow was finished a pimply faced young woman approached me with outstretched hand. "One dollar deposit, please", she chirped, and I not having any dollar . . . left this "homework" place

and also my day's work to its benefit. No. 3: I furnished a sample, received 75 cents' worth of work, and on delivery 15 cents was taken off for a bow for which I did not get any material, being accused of theft, although not directly. ❜

artisans still accounted for 60 per cent of the industrial labour force as late as the 1860s. Nevertheless, foreign observers were contemptuous of their survival. A British Embassy report from Vienna dated January 1858 sketched a dismal picture of a stagnant society enmired in a morass of benighted regulation: 'Each workman, from the day of his apprenticeship, may be said to be bound to one narrow branch of trade, from which there is no escape. If, later in life, he finds his tastes or

instincts draw him in another direction, he must not follow them, unless he is willing again to commence life over. If he perceives that his business might be readily expanded . . . he is probably obliged to abandon all thoughts of it from finding that he would encroach upon the privilege of some other guild. Nor is patient plodding industry allowed a fair chance. The workman must work for the *meister* and for him alone; for . . . if he venture to work on his own account he at once falls under the lash of the law, and the half-employed tailor or shoemaker who, in his leisure hours, makes and sells a coat or a pair of shoes to support his family commits a punishable offence. No one can open a shop without a licence . . . The licence also, when granted, only authorises him to sell a certain class of articles arbitrarily determined upon . . . and, above all, if in the town where he is established, general trade is declining, or his own branch of it is overloaded, he has no power of moving and setting up somewhere else. . . .'

REDUNDANCY AND OPPORTUNITY

The new technologies did sometimes sweep away a specialised skill quite suddenly. The advent of cheap, efficient sewing machines from the 1850s cut a swathe through the ranks of tailors, for example, particularly those producing uniforms, where the demand for large-scale output with limited variations produced at the lowest price cried out for mass-production methods. Similarly, cheap nails and machines that could drive them accurately into leather wrought havoc among bootmakers skilled in the hand-stitching of uppers to soles. Mechanical saws likewise eliminated the need for much routine cutting work in the furniture and joinery trades.

The greatest sufferers from such innovations were usually those with the least skills, most easily imitated by a mechanical process. Often these were 'outworkers' in rural areas, women or peasants working part-time who were more likely to seek alternative employment than to attempt organised resistance in defence of their traditional skill.

But new technologies also created new opportunities. Cheaper tiles eroded the market for the thatcher's skills, for instance. In France, however, railways linking the Midi to Paris, the single largest market for alcohol, stimulated the production of *vin ordinaire*. And so the French thatcher – his market eroded by cheaper tiles, or the wheelwright, struggling as better-surfaced roads meant fewer repairs – might well choose to quit his traditional business on the fringe of the capital. Instead, he might turn his tools and premises into cash and try to join the *petite bourgeoisie* as *proprietaire* of one of hundreds of small bars opening in every working-class quarter to distribute cheap drink from the South.

It was in the great metropolitan centres, Paris, Vienna and London, that artisans survived

HIGH ART Sèvres porcelain represented the highest standards of traditional craftsmanship, the product of a long and complex manufacturing process, depicted in an 18th-century French engraving.

best. Monsieur Audiganne, author of a comparative study of industrial progress published in Paris in 1856, offered his readers a superbly chauvinistic explanation for the continuing superiority of Parisian manufactures in the face of British technological advances: 'It is quite remarkable to see Parisian manufacture remain unrivalled . . . in all the arts where good taste is an essential condition of success . . . It is always public taste which determines tastes in manufacture . . . Perfection in the industrial arts derives then from the very principles which constitute the character of the people . . . Thus the superiority of Paris in the sphere of artistic industries is easily explained by its role in the general development of civilisation.'

The Paris of 1870 had an industrial labour force of some 400 000. Of these 115 000 worked in clothing and textiles, in garrets and sweatshops rather than factories; 110 000 were employed in making jewellery, furniture and other luxury products; 100 000 worked in the building industry; 41 000 were

CALLING CARD A maker of playing cards brandishes the tools of her trade.

in food-processing and 34 000 were in printing. The Faubourg Sainte-Antoine was still clearly an artisan *quartier* at that date, like London's Clerkenwell, with its locksmiths and gunsmiths, clockmakers, jewellers, and manufacturers of scientific and navigational instruments and medical equipment.

THE ARTISAN AS HERO

Even as the artisan was increasingly forced to struggle for survival, his class as a whole remained a symbol of independence and a model for the factory worker or casual labourer. By and large, artisans drank less, wasted less, quarrelled less and saved more than unskilled workers. They supported their own newspapers and organised lecture courses for their own self-improvement. They were

CRUSADES A British union banner (above) shows the worker as Hercules wrestling with the Serpent of Capitalism – 'Until All Destitution, Prostitution and Exploitation Is Swept Away'. A French factory walkout in 1870 (right).

PAUL REVERE: THE ARTISAN AS OPPORTUNIST

PAUL REVERE (1735-1818) is known to Americans as the patriot hero whose exploits in the Revolutionary War were immortalised in poetry by Henry W. Longfellow. In April 1775, while acting as a horseback messenger for the revolutionary leaders, he managed to alert them to British troop movements and save them from arrest.

But the less dramatic, commercial side of his life shows how, in the expanding economy of 18th-century North America, a skilled artisan could rise to become a substantial man of business. Born in Boston of French Huguenot ancestry, Revere was apprenticed to his father, Apollos De Revoire, to learn silversmithing. This was one of the crafts in which the industrious community of Boston excelled. By the age of 30, Revere had extended his range to engraving on copper plates and also revealed a talent for savage political cartooning.

The need to support an ever-growing family, however, led him to diversify his skills even more: he became a maker of surgical instruments, a retailer of spectacles and even a replacer of missing teeth. Revere went on to design the first currency of the revolutionary American regime, the first official seal of the colonies, and the seal still used by his native Massachusetts. War when it came in 1775 gave him the opportunity to learn still more skills: he became an expert in gunpowder and set up as the revolutionaries' chief manufacturer of this much-needed commodity. After the war he opened a foundry and invented a process for rolling sheet copper. In 1808, he supplied the copper plates used to make boilers for the steamboats pioneered by his countryman Robert Fulton.

OUTRAGE A Paul Revere engraving depicts the 'Boston Massacre' of 1770 – a confrontation during the build-up to the Revolutionary War.

---

more regular in attendance at worship, and more consistently concerned with the education, training and advancement of their offspring. As the French printer Martin Bernard put it in the revolutionary year 1848: 'In general workers conceived of their emancipation in only one manner and that is to become a bourgeois, that is to say to become the owner of a workshop and the tools of a trade.'

Another way in which the artisan under pressure managed to survive was by travelling much farther afield for his work. In 1913 it was observed in Belgium that, in remote parts of the country, where housing was more readily available than work: '. . . every quarter of an hour, from the beginning of dusk till well into the night, trains follow trains . . . and at all the villages along the line set down troops of workmen – masons, plasterers . . .

carpenters with their toolbags on their backs . . . some of them obliged to travel 60 or 70 miles [96 or 112 km] to reach their homes. . . .'

In general, though, the artisan had a settled home and a heritage of organisational experience; he was also usually literate. As a result, he was better placed than the unlettered, often nomadic, labourer to fight for his interests. He did this through the new-fangled unions which were replacing the guilds or by the time-honoured method of riot. In France it was the artisans – notably printers, bakers and building craftsmen – who provided the largest contingents on the revolutionary barricades in 1830, 1848 and 1870-1. In Britain it was the skilled artisan who was the backbone of the reform movement Chartism in the 1830s and 40s and the non-violent 'New Model Unionism' of the 1850s, which eschewed utopianism

RESISTING THE MACHINE: THE LUDDITES

CAPTAIN SWING Ned Ludd's rural equivalent, Captain Swing, led attacks on threshing machines that threatened winter employment.

THE ORIGIN of the word 'Luddite', now synonymous with blind opposition to technological progress, lies in an outbreak of machine smashing in England in 1811. It began in Nottinghamshire and spread to the neighbouring Midland counties of Leicestershire and Derbyshire, then to Yorkshire, Lancashire and Cheshire. Claiming to be under the command of one 'Captain', 'General', or 'Ned' Ludd – a mythical figure, allegedly domiciled in Sherwood Forest – the Nottingham Luddites targeted old machines that they said were being abused to produce shoddy stockings with untrained labour, ruining the market and the reputation of their craft:

*Let the wise and the great lend their
    aid and advice
Nor e'er their assistance withdraw
Till full fashioned work at the old
    fashioned price
Is established by custom and law.*

A wall of silence frustrated government efforts to hunt the machine breakers with troops, so Parliament passed a bill to make the smashing of stocking frames a hanging offence. The North was also patrolled by 12 000 soldiers, a larger army than Wellington had taken with him to Portugal to fight the French.

In Lancashire and Cheshire the Luddites went for power looms, and in wool-making Yorkshire for shearing machines. Swinging a hammer nicknamed 'Great Enoch', they chanted their defiance:

*Great Enoch still shall lead the van,
Stop him who dare! Stop him who
    can!*

Hunger was a powerful motive as well as hatred of mechanisation, and several machine-wrecking incidents were accompanied by food riots. In Cheshire, 14 Luddites were sentenced to death, although only two were executed. Seventeen were hanged in Yorkshire, and eight transported. Lancashire saw four executed for burning a mill and four for forcing dealers to sell food at cheap rates. Luddite-type outbreaks also occurred in France in 1819, in Saxony in 1846 and 1848, and in Barcelona between 1852 and 1854.

in favour of detailed negotiation over piece rates and wage differentials. Skilled engineers tended to make skilled strikers, choosing their moment carefully: a dispute in the spring, for example, would catch an employer with a full order book and less blackleg labour to fall back on than in winter; furthermore, the strikers' families would be less vulnerable to shortages of food, clothes or fuel.

LABOUR ON THE MARCH A parade of striking dockers in London in 1889. Such unskilled men organised themselves into unions a generation later than artisans.

FAMILY AND HOME LIFE

A stationmaster poses with his family outside his company-provided house – but the worlds of work and home were becoming increasingly divorced from one another. The Industrial Revolution undermined the family as a home-based team in which parents and children often worked together to earn their livelihood. Family life was more about consumption – and reproduction. Against a background of economic uncertainty, domestic life was idealised as a refuge and a source of comfort and pride.

COURTSHIP AND LOVE

Partnership for life remained the ideal for most men and women, even among those

who dispensed with an actual wedding ceremony. In practice, the hazards of childbirth,

disease and accident often meant that marriages were, indeed, 'until death do us part'.

IN 1861-2 the British *Macmillan's Magazine* published an 'Autobiography of a Navvy' in which an anonymous workman gave vivid details of his courtship and marriage. 'When I was at work at Baldock, in Hertfordshire, about ten years ago, I lodged at a public house. Just opposite lived a young woman, a strawplaiter, who I used to notice many a time, though she did not so much as know me by sight . . . Now I made up my mind to marry this girl . . . Well, I left Baldock after a bit and had never spoken to Anne but once, and that was one evening when I chanced to meet her taking a walk. "So you're out for a walk young woman?" I says to her.

' "Yes, I am," says she, and that was all that passed between us . . . She was the cleanest-looking girl, as I thought, in all the town.'

He then went away for a few months, living 'as steady as possible all the whole time, and [saving] up £4 15s on purpose to marry upon, though I'd never even asked her about it. . . .' After his return, he 'kept on walking with her for about five weeks and we settled to be married the next fair-day – and so we were. It was a very quiet wedding; but they came with a drum and an old tin kettle to give us the rough music. Some people tell you it's unlucky to marry; but all I can say is that it's the luckiest day's work that I ever done in my life. . . .'

RAILWAY PROPRIETY These railway supervisors' 'decent' clothes and neat gardens proclaim their owners' self-respect, despite flimsy huts for homes.

In courtship at least, the poor had an advantage over the rich. While the middle and upper classes tended to be more calculating, weighing up the various claims of beauty, brains, breeding and bank balance, the poor were able to give freer rein to the tugs of mutual attraction. And yet even the propertyless rarely married on impulse alone. In most parts of Europe and North America, the average age at which people got married was in their mid-twenties – although it was usually higher in hard times when men worried more about money and employment prospects. By that time,

A NAVVY'S LIFE
The 'navigators' who dug Britain's canals in the 1790s were hard-drinking nomads. Their successors, building the railways a century later (left), were more orderly but still lived in all-male camps.

IN COMMAND A French middle-class wife gives instructions to her cook. Housewives had to be good managers.

both men and women had gained some experience of life and were more likely to know what qualities made a good marriage partner. At the same time, town life widened the choice of partners (for poor and rich alike). Teenage unions were rare unless pregnancy hastened a couple to the altar.

Working-class men looked for a partner in good health, preferably with household skills. Domestic servants were highly regarded, because they usually acquired a good training and education with their employers. Women looked for 'steadiness' in a man, which meant that he would be a good 'provider' and have no more than the average propensity for drink and violence. If either partner had built up savings, people took it as further evidence of a capacity to 'manage' – one of the best guarantees of a successful marriage.

COMING, MADAM! A London maid negotiates the stairs, tray in hand. Servants worked from before their employers awoke until after they had gone to bed.

A PHILADELPHIA LAWYER ON AMERICAN WOMANHOOD

THE US lawyer Charles J. Ingersoll was an ardent patriot, who deeply resented European assumption of cultural superiority. In 1810, he published an anonymous account of his native country.

❻ Marriages in the United States are contracted early and generally from disinterested motives. With very few exceptions they are sacred . . . The intercourse of the sexes is more familiar, without vice, than in any other part of the world; to which circumstance may, in great measure, be attributed the happy footing of society. This intercourse, in some countries, is confined, by cold and

YES, MY DEAR? The forthright views and conduct of American wives often shocked European visitors to the USA.

haughty customs . . . in others, from opposite causes, it is unrestrained, voluptuous, and depraved. In the United States, it is free, chaste and honourable . . . North America is now that happy mean, when well educated and virtuous women enjoy the confidence of their husbands, the reverence of their children, and the respect of society . . . and as the company of virtuous women is the best school for manners, the Americans, without as high a polish as some Europeans acquire, are distinguished for a sociability and urbanity, that all nations, even the most refined, have not attained. ❾

Women were under more pressure to accept a husband, than men to take a wife. Equally, women might also be expected to risk dalliance with men in the hope of catching one. For a man, marriage remained an option so long as his physical stamina, and therefore earning power, held out. A property-less woman past childbearing age faced only the bleak prospect of living as a perpetual servant – either paid in the home of a stranger, or unpaid in the household of a relative.

Engagements usually lasted no more than a few months or even weeks, while the couple saved up enough money to buy basic furnishings. In major cities, couples also quite often lived together without being formally married. City-dwellers were often migrants, detached from the family networks they had been born into and more tolerant of 'irregular' liaisons than village communities were. If cou-

THE COMFORTABLE CHAIR

Industry brought a new experience to many families – that of sitting comfortably. Mass-produced springs and cushions of horsehair or wool combings meant that people, who had previously made do with a wooden 'Windsor' chair at best, could aspire to padded easy chairs, divans or even sofas.

ples did decide to get married, it often happened after their first baby had been conceived or born – or even later in the relationship. Four-fifths of the silk-workers who married in Lyons in France in 1844 already had children, upon whom the ceremony bestowed a belated legitimacy.

THE BENEFITS OF BUNDLING

In some sparsely populated areas – such as New England before the American Revolution – the shortage of potential marriage partners encouraged the custom of 'bundling'. This covered a range of activities. At its most lax a girl, or even her

WASH AND PAY IN GERMANY A production team (left) at the Dusseldorf Persil factory in 1908. It is payday, and skilled workers queue up on the factory floor at the AEG engineering works in Berlin in 1911.

ON PARADE Middle and upper-class families display domestic harmony in London's Kensington Gardens after church on Sunday morning.

parents if they were desperate to marry her off, put a light in her bedroom window as a sign that she was available. A passing male might then enter, via the window, and after spending the night with her, move on, if he wished to dally no longer. What happened between them was up to the girl to control – knowing that her father and brothers were only a scream away if needed.

At its most ritualised, bundling involved a known suitor who would be formally tucked up in bed with the girl by her parents. Both the young people remained partially clothed. In the most rigorously controlled encounters, girls wore a 'bundling stocking' (a tight-fitting body-length tube of cloth) or had their ankles tied together, and were separated from their partner by a bolster, or even a length of wood, laid down the bed between them. Some girls stitched up their garments at strategic points or constructed hidden defences of pins and needles. Subject to these constraints, the young couple were left alone to get to know one another.

PERMISSION TO MARRY

In central and eastern Europe, marriage for poor people was hedged about with legal, as well as social, restrictions until well into the 19th century. In the 1860s, the English journalist Henry Mayhew was staggered to find in Saxony that men were forbidden by law to marry until they were 24. In addition to this, common workmen had to petition the local town council for permission to marry and prove that they were in stable employment. The town council also had the right to refuse marriage to the 'imbecile', deaf and dumb – but not to the blind, crippled or consumptive.

The wedding ceremony itself was usually very brief, but was followed by a feast which went on

until midnight and was accompanied by numerous age-old rites, one of which scandalised the normally imperturbable Mayhew: 'One of the gentlemen disappears quietly under the table and removes a garter from the leg of every one of the ladies present, it being the custom with the damsels on such occasions to wear bright ribbons expressly for this part of the ceremony. The ribbon garters are then handed up above the table and cut into small pieces for each of the gentlemen to wear at his buttonhole.' This custom was 'practised at the entertainments even of the wealthier classes, and indeed the ancient custom is not omitted at the wedding of royal personages!'

Middle-class customs were more sedate and included much longer engagements. The man might

FOR THE GREAT DAY An English bride-to-be chooses material for her wedding gown. 'Virginal' white became conventional in the later 19th century.

THE RECEPTION The bride and groom salute guests and relatives before a wedding feast in rural France.

have to complete an extended professional training as a lawyer, physician or architect, or wait upon the death of an older man to secure an inheritance, promotion or preferment, or build up a business until 'the trade could carry two'. This process often lasted years or even a decade. Employers, moreover, as well as fathers, were quite prepared to frustrate a marriage if they considered it premature or ill-advised. The British novelist William Makepeace Thackeray, an easy-going parent on the whole, nevertheless warned one of his daughters off 'a penniless clergyman with one lung'. In extreme cases, fathers did not scruple at dispatching their daughters to temporary exile with distant relatives.

The options for an unmarried woman of the propertied classes, although materially less harsh, were emotionally quite as barren as those facing her sisters among the poor. The most frequent refuge was to become a governess or 'lady companion' to another, richer lady – both of them ambiguous positions at best, above the rank of servant but never bringing true equality with one's employer, and exposed to countless petty slights each day. Women with capital might open a shop, boarding house or school, though such ventures were vulnerable to the fluctuations of a volatile economy. In Catholic countries there was also the option of becoming a nun.

Only in the last third of the 19th century did the situation begin to brighten significantly, as the expansion of bureaucracies and school systems, the growth of department stores, hospitals and hotels, and the advent of the telephone and typewriter, opened up a new range of employment opportunities for the educated single woman.

MATCHMAKING AND DOWRIES

For the French, courtship remained more ritualised than in the Anglo-American world, though many French rites did pass over into other countries – as the English adoption of the words *debutante*, *fiancée*, *chaperone* and *trousseau* imply.

Politics and religion figured more prominently

ONLOOKERS Bystanders enjoy the glamour of a middle-class wedding. A French cartoon, showing a sack of cash in a bridal veil, satirises the priorities in fashionable marriages.

in French people's choice of partners, and dowries were far more significant. The indifference of the English-speaking world (Ireland apart) to the matter of dowries – where the bride brought her husband a sum of money on marriage – was a constant source of wonderment to the French. For them, the dowry system enabled newly rich families to ally themselves with more established ones, by marrying their daughters to well-born but underpaid bureaucrats or army officers.

Matchmaking was an important occupation for anxious mothers, romantically minded spinsters and strategically placed cousins. In France, seasonal celebrations, major religious festivals, summer picnics and excursions all offered possible settings for trial introductions. Young men frequently initiated proceedings by approaching a girl's parents through the good offices of a former classmate or colleague at work. If the proposal was accepted, the man's parents then approached the woman's to formalise the engagement, which the two families signified to the world by meeting over dinner at the home of the future bride. Even after their engagement, middle-class couples met only in the presence of a chaperone and conducted any correspondence under the surveillance of the girl's mother.

The two families, meanwhile, worked out the details of the dowry in a formal marriage contract, which was signed in the presence of a notary. Another ritual was for the bride and her parents to gather together a trousseau, symbolising the girl's acceptance of domestic responsibilities. A modest trousseau might consist of three dozen each of items such as sheets, pillowcases, tablecloths, napkins and serving aprons; a lavish one would consist of the same items by the gross.

A church wedding ceremony in many Catholic countries, such as France, could cost the equivalent of a year's salary for a young civil servant. In theory, this was borne by the groom, while the bride's parents paid for the attendant hospitality – which might be spread over two or three days. In practice, the bride's father often discreetly bore most or all of the costs. From the 1830s onwards, the celebrations were customarily followed by a honeymoon – a habit that started in England. Italy – land of Romeo and Juliet – was the most favoured destination, until it was displaced by what were considered to be more exotic locations in Scandinavia towards the end of the century.

MAKING DO IN MARRIAGE

Once married, earning was the husband's responsibility; 'managing' was the wife's. For working-class women, this involved cooking, cleaning, mending and looking after the children, but also adding to the family income whenever possible. There were many ways of doing this: minding children or an invalid for other labouring families; taking in washing;

HOMEWORK A mother and her children in London's East End work together making party streamers. An illustration from a French magazine shows a couple driven to suicide by drink, drudgery and debt.

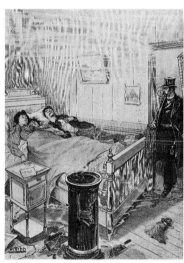

GENTLEMAN FARMING The wife of a prosperous English farmer poses in her pony and trap, while her son straddles his pony. The maid has a uniform but the boys and labourers are dressed for rough work.

seasonal harvest work such as picking fruit or hops; or home-based craft work, such as knitting, strawplaiting or making lace, soft toys, quilts, artificial flowers or cardboard boxes.

The wife of a labourer, rural or urban, had a hard life. It were even tougher for the partner, married or not, of a man – such as a soldier – whose job kept him wandering. Army hierarchies usually ignored soldiers' 'women', unless they were married to NCOs or rankers of long service and conspicuously good conduct. Women who were recognised were expected to act as unpaid washerwomen and nurses; if bereaved, they usually had no more security than the hope of a one-off gratuity from a humane colonel or the proceeds of a collection if the husband had been popular with his comrades.

Marriages often broke down when hard times became harder still, driving men from their homes to look for work elsewhere. Some never returned. Until the later 19th century, most would have been illiterate, and that combined with the prohibitively high cost of postage prevented them from keeping in touch with their families by letter.

The death of a wife, through childbirth, accident or disease, would almost inevitably disperse her family, except in settled communities where the widower could turn to a female relative for help with domestic chores and childminding. More usually the children would be fostered out to relatives, and the man would move into lodgings or take to the road.

Only in old age did women from the poorest classes tend to have an advantage over men. This was largely because their domestic skills, as cooks, nurses or nannies, still had some marketable value, whereas a worn-out labourer had nothing to offer. Old women were almost always less troublesome, too, than men. Many younger wives, especially those whose living standards and aspirations were rising in the late 19th century, hesitated to take in elderly male relatives whose manners, speech, dress or penchant for drink, snuff or gambling, betrayed the coarseness of their origins and jeopardised a family's hard-won claim to 'respectability'.

MANAGING THE HOUSEHOLD

In the middle classes, most people assumed that a husband would oversee his wife's conduct of domestic affairs. In practice, however, wives usually had a fairly free hand, acting as stewards of the household, organising its daily routines, disciplining the children and managing expenditure. Unlike their working-class counterparts, middle-class wives also had the task of ensuring that their servants were diligent, honest, sober and chaste and, as far as possible, worked as a harmonious team.

At the same time, factory production, leading to a growing separation of home and workplace, destroyed traditional household structures in which apprentices and employees had been considered almost as family members. In Germany, social critics noted that middle-class wives, freed from the need to supervise their husband's employees, had fallen prey to a 'reading rage' and wasted hours curled up on sofas with piles of romantic novels.

The positive side of this leisure was an enrichment of domestic life, through musical evenings, play readings and hobbies designed to beautify the home with needlework or knick-knacks. The ceremonies surrounding a German Christmas – which figures such as Queen Victoria's German husband, Prince Albert, and Charles Dickens helped to popularise in Britain – also epitomised this cult of family life. (It was no coincidence that Germany had the world's largest and most inventive toy industry.) Birthdays and, in Catholic countries, Saints' Days offered opportunities for celebrations, with lavish meals and presents, especially for children.

As home life was so highly valued, visitors to America were appalled by the number of families living not in homes, but hotels. In 1844, one in six of Chicago's permanent residents lived in a hotel, and one in four in a boarding house or with an employer. The English feminist Barbara Bodichon attributed the popularity of the hotel to young wives' inability to cope with expensive and domineering servants: 'It is natural that the American matron of 17 or 18 should seek refuge from this domestic terrorism in the gilded saloons of the St Nicholas or St Charles [hotels] or whatever other Saint may offer his protection for 2¹/₂ dollars a day.'

THE CRECHE A Swiss painting shows a young woman 'minding' children from a poor district of Berne. The mothers were thus freed for work outside the home.

Complete marriage breakdown among the middle classes was rare. Obtaining a formal divorce was an expensive and lengthy procedure; living parallel lives was a far simpler way of dealing with unhappiness. Divorce, when it did occur, was most frequent among members of the armed services and colonial officials, for whom overseas postings frequently led to prolonged separations and 'irregular' liaisons. Generally speaking, the smaller and more stable the community, the lower the incidence of breakdown. For a man, divorce posed not only practical problems of keeping up a household without a wife to supervise it, but also the risk of damaging his public reputation.

A woman, too, had every incentive to maintain even the barest façade of a marriage. On her own, she would have little prospect of financial independence, since she was unlikely to have skills or qualifications of value in the marketplace. As custody of children was nearly always awarded to the father, she would lose them as well. In cases of overt and sustained cruelty, she might be taken in by a kindly male relative. For the rest, most countries' legal systems implicitly condoned male infidelity, while adultery by females almost invariably constituted unquestionable grounds for divorce, followed by total social ostracism.

CHILDHOOD AND UPBRINGING

For all the horrors of the growing industrial cities, many people, including workers, had more

money than ever before. At the same time, younger marriages and improved

diet and hygiene produced a surge in the proportion of children and young people.

CHARLES DICKENS was less than enthusiastic about the birth in 1852 of his ninth surviving child Edward: 'on the whole I could have dispensed with him'. Yet few writers did more to idealise the joys of home and hearth, or to express compassion for the many children of his time born without secure family backgrounds. Dickens was a keen supporter of London's Foundling Hospital, which was only a few hundred yards from his first marital home in Bloomsbury's Doughty Street. He attended Sunday chapel services there regularly. Tattycoram, the foundling in *Little Dorrit*, is named in affectionate honour of the hospital's founder, Captain Thomas Coram.

A century before, the Swiss philosopher Jean-Jacques Rousseau had advanced the novel notion that children were naturally virtuous, and should

HOME DELIVERY A middle-class French mother gives birth amid the comfort of home. Childhood presents a different face for London street urchins. As many as 20 000 homeless children may have lived rough on the streets of the British capital around 1850.

HOMES FOR FOUNDLINGS

ARGE CITIES had a high concentration of servants, criminals apprentices, soldiers and casual labourers – and thus had a higher than average share of single people. The resulting sexual activity inevitably resulted in unwanted children.

In 1833 alone, 128 000 newborn French children were abandoned by their parents. In France as a whole, between 20 and 30 per cent of children born each year were illegitimate, and in Paris the proportion stood between 30 and 40 per cent. Luckless infants dispatched to its *Maison de la Couche* – 'House of Confinement' – faced a grim prospect. On average half would die within three months of admission and another fifth before their first birthday. Some Italian orphanages had mortality rates of 90 per cent. As late as 1858 a report to the Massachusetts state government on its 'Public Charitable Institutions' estimated that 'probably not more than 3 per cent of those orphans, of an age less than one year when they enter the almshouses, live'.

EXPENDABLE Orphan children (below left) were employed by sweeps to climb inside chimneys and clear them of soot. In contrast, a brood of well-dressed children (below right) is paraded for public admiration.

Efforts to establish a Foundling Hospital in London were initially opposed, on the grounds that an orphanage would encourage immorality. However, a royal charter was finally granted in 1739 to establish a 'Hospital for the Maintenance and Education of Exposed and Deserted Young Children'. Its supporters were to include the painters William Hogarth and Joshua Reynolds, the sculptor Michael Rysbrack and the composer George Frideric Handel, all of whom were active fund raisers. Admissions to the institution were restricted to the first-born of an unmarried mother of previously good character. Ailing infants were

**SUBSTITUTE MOTHERS
French nuns (above) care for infants abandoned on the steps of their convent. 'Fallen women' (left), cast on the streets with their offspring, were often forced into prostitution to feed them.**

refused admission but, even so, a third of those who were accepted died in their first year. It became customary, therefore, to send inmates to foster parents in the countryside until they were five, when they returned to the capital for their education.

Despite this precaution fewer than a third of the hospital's children survived long enough to take up an apprenticeship or a position in domestic service. Strictly segregated by gender within the institution, the ones who failed to make it to the outside world were kept apart even in death, and were buried in separate cemeteries.

FILTH A mother and child (far left) squat in squalor in Glasgow, second city of the world's greatest empire. Britain's infant mortality in 1900 was no lower than it had been in 1840. Left: A Breton wet nurse and infant in 1899.

be gently stimulated into realising their full potential. Views in the Anglo-Saxon world, however, still tended to a conservative belief in the Biblical injunction that sparing the rod would spoil the child.

In many places, boys were still preferred to girls (as they had been for centuries), and midwives and priests throughout Europe knew that fathers paid their various fees cheerfully for a male birth, grudgingly for a girl. In France the registration of male offspring was cause for congratulation from the local mayor, because it meant another soldier '*pour la patrie*'.

But, despite age-old prejudices, times were changing, with parents becoming more deeply involved in the upbringing of their children. This could be seen in the decline in the practice of wet-nursing. In the 1780s, some four-fifths of Parisian babies were shipped off to the countryside to be wet-nursed. By the 1870s, the custom was limited to the lower middle classes, among whom wives had to be free to assist in the running of the family business. Poor mothers started using feeding-bottles made from the teats of cows or goats and boiled in limewater from the early 19th century onwards. Ceramic bottles became available from the 1870s.

European visitors to the United States found parent-child relationships strikingly different from what they were used to at home. In the 1790s, a Polish observer, Julian Niemcewicz, described the behaviour of an American general's five-year-old daughter: '. . . a spoiled child, as are most American children. One hears her sometimes say to her mother "you damn'd bitch". The least inconvenience that she encounters makes unhappiness for the whole household'.

The British Harriet Martineau was more favourably impressed in the 1830s, finding American children refreshingly bright and articulate. In Baltimore she attended a 'juvenile ball'. 'If I had at home gone in among eighty or a hundred little people between the ages of eight and sixteen, I should have extracted little more than "Yes, ma'am" and "No, ma'am". At Baltimore a dozen boys and girls crowded round me, questioning, discussing, speculating . . . in a way which enchanted me.'

Tight swaddling (thought to help babies' limbs to grow straight) was still practised in France, Italy and Germany as late as the 1890s. At the same time, continental prejudices against washing babies

SURVIVAL RATES

Only 78 out of every 100 newborn Swedish babies in 1760 reached their first birthday; 66 reached their fifth birthday, and 57 their 20th. The statistics were fairly typical of any society not yet touched by industrialism. Some 225 years – and an industrial revolution – later, 78 babies would live to be 68; 66 would get to 74, and 57 would celebrate their 77th birthday. Life expectancy not only increased; it also equalised among the different countries of the Western world. In 1760, the average Swede could expect to live to 36, the average Frenchman only to 25. Nowadays, the respective figures are 74 and 72.

MOTHER'S RUIN An exhausted woman
quietens her baby with gin.
Opium-based 'medicines' were
also used as pacifiers. Without adequate sterilisation,
feeding bottles could be a source of infection.

contrasted strongly with British beliefs about the virtues of cold-water baths and sea-bathing from an early age. Constipation was regarded with horror and was tackled with regular doses of laxative. At British boarding schools, canings were a routine aspect of discipline.

For most working-class children, childhood was over by the time they were eight or ten years old. If legislation in many countries banned them from full-time work in mines or factories after the mid 19th century, it did little to keep them out of smaller workshops or off the land, where even the smallest could scare crows or pick up stones.

Joseph Arch, founder of Britain's first successful trade union for agricultural labourers, knew from his own harsh experience that for a young lad farm work was anything but idyllic: 'If [a boy] got past the bird-scaring stage he had the carter and the ploughman to contend with and their tenderest mercies were cruel. They used their tongues and their whips and their boots on him so freely, that it is no exaggeration to say that the life of [a farm boy] was not a whit better than that of a plantation nigger boy.' In the USA, the census of 1900 revealed that there were almost 700 000 children aged between 10 and 15 in non-agricultural employment. Some were out of public view – in Pennsylvania coal mines, Midwestern glassworks, or Carolina cotton mills – but thousands worked on city streets, as delivery boys or in stores.

For the children of middle-class homes, on the

other hand, childhood became ever more extended and protected as the 19th century progressed. Parents agonised over their upbringing as a new breed of self-appointed experts emerged to offer their opinions on the right combinations of indulgence and severity. *Domestic Education*, a manual published in 1840 by Herman Humphrey of Amherst College, Massachusetts, took the uncompromising line that 'in the family organisation there is but one model, for all times and all places . . . Every father is the constituted head and ruler of his household. God has made him the supreme earthly legislator over his children'. *The Mother's Book*, published in Boston in 1831 by Lydia Maria Child, a prolific writer,

MAN'S WORK, BOY'S WORK A boy takes centre stage in
this New York sweatshop of the 1880s.

TEENAGE TERRORS IN LONDON'S CAPITAL

MOST ENGLISH CITIES had workhouses with 'casual wards' where itinerants could seek shelter overnight. But the casual wards also became convenient shelters and way-stations for a class of youthful marauders, estimated in 1848 to be 16 000 strong. An experienced Poor Law official in south London gave an account of their character and way of life:

❝ The largest number were 17 years old . . . [They] had generally run away from either parents or masters . . . [and] were mostly shrewd and acute . . . These lads are mostly distinguished by their aversion to continuous labour of any kind . . . They are physically stout, healthy lads, and certainly not emaciated or sickly . . . When in London they live in the daytime by holding horses and carrying parcels from the steam piers and railway termini. Some loiter about the markets in the hope of a job, and others may be seen in the streets picking up bones and rags, or along the waterside searching for pieces of old metal or anything that may be sold . . . They have nearly all been in prison more than once . . . They are the most dishonest of all thieves, having not the least respect for the property of even the members of their own class. They are very stubborn and self-willed . . . They are particularly fond of amusements . . . Sometimes they will elect a chairman and get up a regular debate and make speeches from one side of the ward to the other . . . [while] others delight in singing comic songs, especially those upon the workhouse and gaols . . . They are perfectly organised, so that any regulation affecting their comforts or interests becomes known among the whole body in a remarkably short space of time . . . [They] form one of the most restless, discontented, vicious and dangerous elements of society. ❞

ON'Y A SHILLIN', MISTER! Children such as this cloth seller in London's Petticoat Lane were often employed to sell goods on street corners. British schoolgirls of 1908 are taught to sew both by hand and with a machine.

preached the need to mould a child's character by example: 'The simple fact that your child never saw you angry, that your voice was always gentle, and the expression of your face always kind, is worth a thousand times more than all the rules you can give him about not beating his dog, pinching his brother &c.' But even Mrs Child knew that there were times to draw a line. Her golden rule was 'always punish a child for wilfully disobeying you in the most trifling particular; but never punish him in anger'.

At a national level, international rivalries and crude theories of 'racial dominance' combined to inspire the view that children were not only a sacred trust, but a crucial national asset as well. The first decade of the 20th century witnessed the first production of Sir James Barrie's play *Peter Pan* – the boy who never grew up. But it also saw the

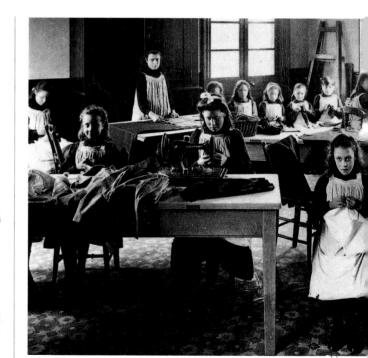

establishment of the Boy Scouts by the British general Sir Robert Baden-Powell in 1908. Many Boy Scouts were to exchange one brown uniform for another in 1914 and perish in Flanders fields.

Family life was, of course, closely bound up with birth control – or the lack of it. Various techniques

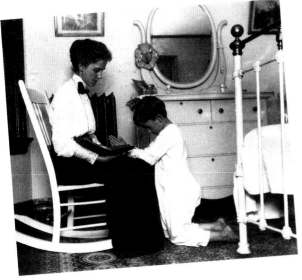

DEVOTIONS An English mother listens to her son's evening prayers. 'Honour thy father and thy mother' was the best known of the Ten Commandments.

for limiting births had been known and practised for centuries. But passing on this knowledge was severely hampered by traditional taboos and the attitude of the Church. Late weaning was one well-known method, which worked to some extent because lactation depresses fertility, particularly in the undernourished. In the 17th century, sheaths made of fish or animal membranes were on sale, but chiefly to prevent the spread of venereal diseases.

LIMITING FAMILIES

The most common methods of contraception, how-ever, were withdrawal, or *coitus interruptus,* and simple abstinence. Others included sponges soaked in disinfectant, or injections of warm water tinged with vinegar. Many French adults were pre-pared to take more drastic and certain steps; the development of antiseptic surgery made removal of the ovaries a relatively safe operation.

Figures for infanticide and abortion are hard to come by, since most cases were kept secret. In France, however, it is known that abortions were generally performed by midwives. Estimates of the annual number in France around 1900 range from 100 000 to 400 000. But the reasons for the abor-tions had changed over the century. Whereas most in the early 1800s had been performed on single women or widows threatened with dishonour, now the clientele consisted largely of married women, concerned to limit the size of their families.

Only in the 1870s and 1880s did reliable rubber condoms become widely available. At first, they were within the reach only of those who could afford to pay for private medical consultations, but by the 1890s postal sales services had been devel-oped. Protestant and Catholic clergy both feared that passion without consequences might lead to a tidalwave of promiscuity. Nevertheless, by 1908, Britain's Registrar General was announcing a fall in fertility, attributing 79 per cent of it to 'deliberate restriction of childbearing'.

A trend towards smaller families greatly en-hanced women's chances of long life. Small fami-lies were a married woman's best guarantee of making it to old age, for childbirth was a far more deadly killer than diseases such as cholera or tuberculosis. Millions of young brides experienced six or seven pregnancies in less than a decade, fol-lowed by rest, at last – under a headstone.

LAST JOURNEY A Danish painting of 1879 shows a child's waterborne funeral. The tiny coffin is being rowed from an island to a mainland churchyard.

HOMES AND HOME LIFE

'A Home of One's Own' was the ideal for people of all classes. But many of

the poor had to share their homes with lodgers, relatives, other families and,

in the 'sweated trades', their own equipment and raw materials.

A S LATE AS 1900, almost 60 per cent of Europe's population lived in communities of 5000 people or less. But the trend to move away from the villages into towns was already well established. A century earlier the proportion had been more than 85 per cent. In the United States, the proportion of the population classified as 'urban' rose from around 10 per cent in 1840 to about 35 per cent by 1890, and more than 45 per cent by 1910.

The typical dwelling of poor country people in Europe in the 1780s was a one-storey building made of whatever materials were most readily available. In well-wooded areas a home would be made of timber, with perhaps a roof of wooden shingles; in mountains, of stone; in warm lowland areas, of sun-baked brick, roofed with kiln-baked tiles; in cooler regions, of wooden laths and wicker,

SCARCELY CELEBRATING A Berlin family work, cook and sleep in the same room. A French silk-worker pauses for soup in an apartment dominated by his loom.

HOMELESS AT THE HOUSE OF GOD   Poor Italians savour free soup on the steps of a convent in Rome.

daubed with mud and dung and roofed with a thatch of straw or reeds.

The floor would almost invariably be of stamped-down dirt, dusty in summer, slippery in winter. Heating would come from an open fire, which was also used for cooking and usually provided the only light at night. In the absence of an oven, cooking was done by roasting over naked flames or boiling in a cauldron. Given the expense of meat – apart from pigs and goats, which could be raised on kitchen waste – thick vegetable-based soups and stews were the most common form of hot food. Window glass would be a rare luxury: shutters were used instead. There would be neither running water nor artificial lighting, apart from candles or tallow-coated rushlights, too expensive to use on a regular basis. Separate sleeping quarters, where they existed, meant a pile of hay or a straw-stuffed mattress in the roof space. Furniture was minimal and was usually homemade – stools and benches to sit on, chests and rough shelves for storage.

Fastidious French investigators of rural housing in the 1840s recorded conditions of medieval squalor: 'Champagne and Picardy . . . the Limousin, Brittany and the like must be seen and seen up close. You find rooms that serve as kitchen, dining

A PRUSSIAN AGENT IS APPALLED AT AN EXILE'S QUARTERS

THE YEAR was 1851. The address was 28 Dean Street, Soho, London (now an Italian restaurant) in which two upstairs rooms were home to M—, his wife, his three children and an adult maid. M— was Karl Marx.

❛ M— lives in one of the worst, therefore one of the cheapest, quarters of London. He occupies two rooms. The one looking out on the street is the parlour and the bedroom is at the back. In the whole apartment there is not one clean and solid piece of furniture. A seller of secondhand goods would be ashamed to give away such a remarkable collection of odds and ends. When you enter . . . smoke and tobacco fumes make your eyes water so much that for a moment you seem to be groping about in a cavern . . . Everything is dirty and covered with dust, so that to sit down becomes a thoroughly dangerous business. Here is a chair with only three legs, on another the children are playing at cooking . . . This is the one which is offered to the visitor, but the children's cooking has not been wiped away; and if you sit down, you risk a pair of trousers. ❜

POPULATION EXPLOSION

Across the industrialising world, populations grew faster than ever. Scholars dispute the causes – but no one disputes its impact.

MOST BRITISH OBSERVERS in the 18th century took it for granted that economic growth went hand in hand with a rapid growth in population. As the agricultural expert Arthur Young put it in 1770: 'It is employment that creates population . . . Marriages are early and numerous, in proportion to the amount of employment. . . .'

But the rise in population was not confined to Britain, whose economy expanded most dramatically in the 18th century. Between 1751 and 1801, the population of England grew at an average rate of 0.80 per cent per year, about twice as fast as in France or Italy – but slower than in relatively 'backward' East Prussia, Austria and Bohemia.

In the first half of the 19th century, the United States' population grew by 3 per cent annually, helped by immigration from Europe.

Populations were growing fast, but explanations for the growth were not always obvious. Medicine made great advances between 1750 and 1850, but – apart from the conquest of smallpox by vaccination – doctors and hospitals had little impact on the lives of the poor. Lying-in hospitals reduced the number of stillbirths among better-off townspeople by giving access to better facilities than a village midwife could offer. But the women ran a greater risk of contracting puerperal (childbed) fever, normally with fatal results. Not until the mid 19th century

BREADLINE Soup kitchens in Paris. When times were hard, jobless workers and their families were driven to the edge of survival.

did it become clear that doctors were themselves the main source of danger as they habitually passed from dissecting corpses to examining patients without washing, let alone disinfecting, their hands.

One factor, beyond all others,

IN THE CAN Tinned goods – such as peas prepared by the French company Gontier Frères – were widely available by the 1890s. The lavish display outside an English grocer's shop reflects the rising purchasing power of the working class.

STAPLE FOOD **German maids prepare potatoes in a middle-class kitchen of 1889. The potato was also a staple for the working class.**

probably accounts for the general rise in Europe's population: the 'miracle vegetable', the potato. Introduced from South America in the 16th century, its cultivation spread slowly across the north European plain – afflicted at the time by the religious strife of the Thirty Years' War – where peasants valued it as an emergency reserve of nutrition. Another virtue was that the potato could be cultivated with nothing more complicated or expensive than a spade. It survived in poor soil, and thrived on small patches of land, not worth putting down to grain. Area for area, it yielded four times as much food value as wheat.

Maize, also from the New World, was almost as productive. As these two crops become the staple diet of the poor of Europe, any young man with access to an acre of land could contemplate marriage. Marrying sooner than if he had to work and wait for a larger holding, his bride would have a longer period of childbearing. Even more importantly, his better-fed children would have an improved chance of surviving infancy and making it to adulthood.

In the second half of the 19th century, better public hygiene kept the momentum going by reducing mortality. The most important measures were to provide efficient drainage systems and clean water supplies, which dramatically reduced the outbreaks of typhoid, cholera, dysentery and other water-borne diseases.

At the same time, 'model housing' and, later, isolation hospitals in rural areas, helped to diminish tuberculosis. Belated regulation of conditions in mills, mines and other work places reduced work-related accidents and ailments. Inexpensive cotton underwear and cheap soap did their bit, by promoting better personal hygiene.

AND YOU, YOU'RE WELL? **A French cartoon shows Parisian flu sufferers. Cheap carbolic soap improved standards of personal hygiene. Workers in a US processing factory prepare food for packing.**

Design No. 5   Plate No. 23

FRONT ELEVATION.
SCALE.

SECTION
SCALE.

IDEAL HOME US 'balloon-frame' houses relied on mass-produced lumber and standardised builders' pattern books to produce 'individual' homes.

room and bedroom for the whole family . . . They also serve as cellar and attic, and sometimes as stable and barn-yard as well . . . In this room people prepare their food, dis-card wet and sweaty clothing, dry and age cheeses, and store or hang salted meats.'

Even at the end of the 19th century, millions still lived in such conditions in Russia and the Balkans, in the poorer parts of Italy and the Iberian peninsula and in Ireland. By then, however, most country-dwellers in other parts of Europe and North America had acquired wooden or tiled floors, glass windows, pumped water, and some form of oil or kerosene lamp.

In northern Europe, which was both more pros-perous and colder than the rest of the Continent, they would also have an oven or stove made of iron, rag rugs for the floors, upholstered furniture, bedsteads of iron or brass and, usually, a looking-glass, a clock, a galvanised tin bath and an iron mangle with wooden rollers. Those who could af-ford to covered the walls of their rooms with wall-paper and decorated them with cheap engravings,

usually of a patriotic or reli-gious character.

American country-dwellers were already achieving even higher standards of domestic comfort. Willa Cather's novel, *O Pioneers*, chronicles the transformation of Nebraska from the 'Wild Land' of the 1880s to the more settled mid-1890s, when the Swedish hero-ine Alexandra has graduated from a one-room cabin to a gra-cious house filled with elegant knick-knacks and surrounded by a flower garden. She even punctuates her daily routine with telephone calls to neighbours and on Sunday attends a brick-built church complete with electric lighting.

A HOME IN THE CITY

In preindustrial towns and cities the poorest of the poor lived in shacks and shanties: flimsy hovels, built out of scavenged scraps, on patches of waste ground, under bridges or leaning against town walls. The rest of the poor were often crammed

ROWS – NOT ROWS Terraced housing, such as this row in Birmingham, England, economised on materials but also put a premium on neighbourliness. An English project manager and building worker pose for posterity as they test the strength of a new cement.

CROWD SCENES
Parisians queue
for meat. Trams
(right) meant
people could live
beyond walking
distance from
their work places.

into houses originally built for the better-off and later abandoned and sub-divided, to be let room by room for use as 'apartments' or workshops.

There were two major exceptions to this rule. Servants and apprentices lived in the households of their masters, even if young lads often had to make their beds on the kitchen floor or in a backyard stable. The 'respectable' aged poor in Catholic areas often found refuge in religious institutions. In Protestant regions there were almshouses, funded by the charitable endowments of wealthy merchants or town guilds. This was the only type of housing built to a reasonable standard with the urban poor in mind – and a very small and privileged segment of them at that.

Industrialisation, and the growth of towns, created an unprecedented housing crisis for the poor. There were three major responses: subdividing existing properties still further, notably by colonising attics and cellars; speculative building of new properties, usually constructed to the lowest feasible standards; and, finally, provision of 'model dwellings', initially by philanthropic individuals or organisations, latterly by civic governments.

Middle-class housing reflected middle-class values and aspirations: comfort, health, privacy, respectability. Unskilled workers lodged where they could. Skilled workers had more choice, but for most of the 19th century they were still tied to areas within walking distance of their work – that is, areas polluted by the smoke and noise of the in-

dustries that employed them. Cheap 'workmen's fares' on the railways, the arrival of the tram in the 1870s and the development of the 'safety bicycle' in the 1880s allowed people to live farther from their places of work.

As the demand for homes in towns intensified in the first half of the 19th century, speculative builders began to run up gimcrack cottages and tenements on patches of waste ground or outside city boundaries. Others squeezed houses in between or behind the houses of the rich, who were potential customers for working-class services. As the social investigator John Hollingshead remarked in *Ragged London* in 1861: 'From Belgravia to Bloomsbury . . . there is hardly a settlement of leading residences that has not its particular colony of ill-housed poor hanging on to its skirts. Behind the mansion there is generally a stable, and near the stable there is generally a maze of close streets, containing . . . houses let out in tenements. These houses shelter a large number of painters, bricklayers, carpenters and similar labourers with their families, and many laundresses, and charwomen.

THE DOMESTIC GRIND

Technology promised to ease the American housewife's burden of

domestic chores – but mysteriously ended up by multiplying them.

A COMMITMENT TO egalitarian ideals and the relatively high price of labour both meant that in America fewer housewives could delegate their housework to servants than was possible for their European counterparts. An immigrant girl from Norway, for instance, wrote in amazement to her parents that 'here the mistress of the house must do all the work that the cook, the maid and the housekeeper would do in an upper-class family at home'.

As a result, there was a greater demand for products and gadgets to make household work easier. In the course of the 19th century, that demand provided a powerful stimulus to the American economy but,

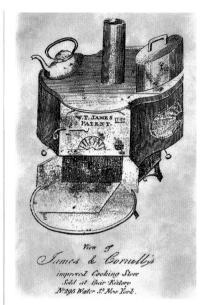

HI-TECH The inventor William T. James patented his cooking stove in 1823. It also heated the kitchen and boiled water for washing.

DOMESTIC ROUND Recipe books such as this one of 1858 gave advice on curing, pickling and preserving. On Sundays, a rigorous calm reigned. The members of this New England family have five Bibles among them.

paradoxically, housewives seldom found that they had any more time on their hands. In fact, the main beneficiary of new household products was the husband.

When the United States first won independence, the majority of white Americans lived in small rural or semi-rural settlements. It was the job of husbands and sons to chop the firewood and haul the water from a stream, spring or well. It was also a man's task to butcher the family's meat and to husk and grind corn to make flour. A century later, most city homes as well as those on the prairies, where timber was scarce, had switched from open fireplaces to stoves, which used less or burned coal. This spelt the end of the male task of chopping wood, while piped or pumped water likewise abolished trudging to the nearest natural source.

In towns, home-killed meat was replaced by a joint from a Chicago meat-packer or a local butcher, and home-ground cornmeal gave way to flour from the mill. This eliminated another male chore but did nothing to diminish the female task in the home, where fires still had to be kept going, dishes, sheets and clothes washed, stews cooked and bread and biscuits baked.

In colonial days, both husband and wife usually 'worked around the house', neither expecting to be paid for their labours; a century later, the typical American husband went 'out to work', for which he was paid, while his wife stayed at home to 'do housework', for which she was not.

The housewife was on a treadmill of increasing expectations. The old-fashioned pot over an open fire made one-dish meals the norm. The stove, with its ovens and separate cooking surfaces, made it possible to produce both a stew and a pie at the same time. And whereas cooking with coarsely ground cornmeal was a swift and simple process, cooking with finely ground wheat flour required yeast and laborious kneading to produce satisfactory results. A French visitor remarked that the Pilgrim Fathers must have landed with a Bible under one arm and a cookery book under the other.

Cake-baking required the time-consuming assembly and preparation of 'store-bought' ingredients (such as grinding down loaves of sugar), as well as great effort to combine them, as in: 'Take eight eggs, beat and strain them and put to them a pound of sugar . . . beat it three quarters of an hour together.' The invention of the egg-beater was offset by the popularity of angel cakes – which required eggs and yolks to be beaten separately, thus doubling the labour.

What was true of food was also true of clothes. Colonial frontiersmen wore much leather, which was never washed. City folk a century later wore cotton shirts and underwear, both of which could be

DOMESTIC DISASTER Makers of 'patent' foodstuffs promised to release the overworked housewife from the consequences of her incompetence.

washed easily – and often. Mill-woven cloth released housewives from spinning and weaving, but not from sewing. City-dwellers expected to have a far larger selection of clothes than their rural ancestors.

If candle-making was a female chore eliminated by oil and gas lamps, cleaning the lamps' glass globes of soot was a new task. Home canning and bottling meant that a wider range of fruits and vegetables could be preserved than before. So, because it could be done, it was done, and another chore was added to the autumn business of making pickles and preserves.

US families of the railway age ate a far more varied diet than their grandparents had, and they were warmer and cleaner at home and in their own persons than any previous generation. Released from the time-consuming chores inseparable from primitive frontier conditions, children were free to go to school, fathers to the factory. Mothers stayed at home – and taught their daughters what they knew.

SHRINE TO HYGIENE This porcelain and copper wonder from the USA even has a thermometer.

WASTE NOT . . . **Many, such as these Parisian 'ragpickers', scraped an existence sorting, selling and recycling growing mountains of discarded goods.**

Each room, with a few exceptions, is the home of a different family.'

Slums far worse than these could be found in the mushroom-growth cities of America, notably Cleveland, St Louis, Boston and Chicago, where detached timber houses intended for a single family were crammed with five or six and had further rows of timber shacks crammed into their backyards. Worst of all was New York where, between 1868 and 1875, an estimated 500 000 people – half the city's population – lived in slums.

Paradoxically, landlords made the highest profits from the most overcrowded properties. In New York in the 1870s the rent per square foot of a slum property was 25-35 per cent higher than that of apartments in the fashionable uptown area. Let to the poorest of the poor, who were in no position to quibble or complain, these apartments received the very minimum of repair or maintenance.

JOHN BULL INSPECTS JEAN-PIERRE

IN 1871, the British Ambassador to Paris wrote this report on the living conditions of the French working classes:

❦ The food of the French workman is, as a general rule, substantially inferior to that to which the Englishman is accustomed. Many a French factory-hand never has anything better for his breakfast than a large slice of common sour bread rubbed over with an onion to give it a flavour. For dinner, some soup, potatoes or carrots, and sometimes a small piece of pork . . . and for their last meal they eat the meat of which their soup was composed. . . . The French have always been renowned for their culinary skill. It is talent peculiar to the whole nation. The very poorest classes possess it. A French man or woman will manufacture a palatable meal out of the very coarsest, and what, to our ideas, may appear even most repulsive, materials. The 'soupe', which is to be met with on every French workman's table, is infinitely preferable to the concoction of hot water, pepper and gravy which the richest millionaire in England is obliged to put up with, if he has to dine at an ordinary English provincial hotel, or even at many an establishment in the metropolis calling itself first-class. . . .

The result of this is, that a French workman can live, even luxuriously, where an Englishman would starve.

Within the last few years the consumption of beer has increased enormously among all classes. Formerly it was almost unknown in France; now it is the common restaurant beverage of the Parisian middle class. The workmen, however, still cling to their wine, the beverage consumed by all classes at home . . . The French are very much addicted to the use of the deleterious spirit called 'absinthe', which has a most injurious effect on their health. The Englishman is at all times too prone to indulge freely in drink, but if he has any regard for his health he will be careful to avoid dram-drinking . . . for, in addition to the adulterated character of these spiritous liquors, the dry climate of France will not permit men to take with impunity the amount of spirit which they could, perhaps, drink in England without any positively injurious effect. ❦

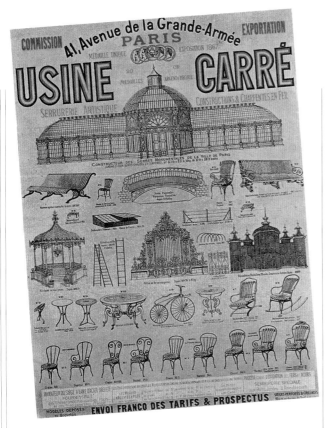

The living conditions which drove French city-dwellers to the barricades in 1830 and 1848 are described in a report drawn up for the municipality of Lille in 1832: 'It is impossible to imagine the

MODEL DWELLINGS A photograph of 1900 shows the Krupps ironworks at Essen, Germany. Krupps workers and their families lived in specially designed housing with traffic-free play space for children.

dwellings of our working classes without seeing them . . . In their dark, underground dens, in their upstairs rooms, which still might be taken for cellars, the atmosphere, however loathsome, is never changed . . . The furniture is mildewed, bedaubed and broken. The windows, always closed, are pasted up with paper so blackened and smoked that the light is unable to penetrate. In some cases the windows are nailed up by the proprietor to prevent the panes of glass from being broken by opening.

'WORKERS' CITIES' IN FRANCE

Under the French Second Empire (1852-70), an attempt was made to address the issue of urban housing through the construction of so-called 'workers' cities', in effect large apartment blocks. A typical example could be found at the great port of Marseilles. An apartment three storeys high contained 150 rooms, each opening onto a long central corridor and furnished with an iron bedstead, a table, two chairs, a cupboard and a looking glass. A large canteen supplied meals at reasonable prices and an attendant doctor gave medical care free. Hot baths were made available every Sunday.

A similar project built in Rouen had 90 apartments and 15 shops to serve the inhabitants; the blocks also had such facilities as gas, flush lavatories, rubbish chutes, a laundry room, an infirmary and, as a nod to the rural roots of most of the tenants – a cider press. The most successful version was in Mulhouse, where the inspiration came from English models. The developers were convinced

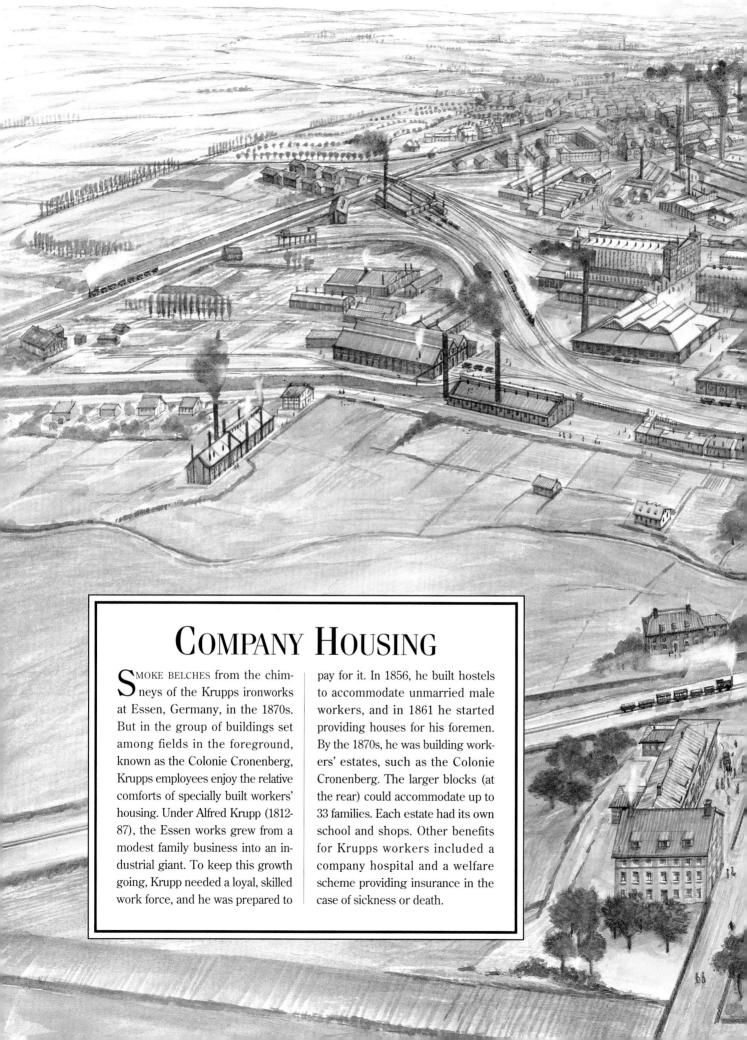

COMPANY HOUSING

Smoke belches from the chimneys of the Krupps ironworks at Essen, Germany, in the 1870s. But in the group of buildings set among fields in the foreground, known as the Colonie Cronenberg, Krupps employees enjoy the relative comforts of specially built workers' housing. Under Alfred Krupp (1812-87), the Essen works grew from a modest family business into an industrial giant. To keep this growth going, Krupp needed a loyal, skilled work force, and he was prepared to pay for it. In 1856, he built hostels to accommodate unmarried male workers, and in 1861 he started providing houses for his foremen. By the 1870s, he was building workers' estates, such as the Colonie Cronenberg. The larger blocks (at the rear) could accommodate up to 33 families. Each estate had its own school and shops. Other benefits for Krupps workers included a company hospital and a welfare scheme providing insurance in the case of sickness or death.

that 'bringing many strange families together under one roof rarely leads to tranquil domestic harmony and may give rise to serious disorders'. So the Mulhouse *cité* was composed not of barrack-like blocks but of detached two-storey houses, each with a cellar, a large room and a kitchen on the ground floor, and three bedrooms, a privy and storage area on the upper floor, plus its own garden. There were also furnished apartments for the unmarried in small blocks of 17 rooms.

Common facilities included child care and medical services, a washhouse, bathhouse and swimming pool, a bakery and a restaurant. By 1895, the development had expanded to house 10000 people, a tenth of the city's entire population.

Late in the day, the middle class began to discover that working-class families were no less fond of privacy than they were. The apartment blocks most easily rented out were those that had a variety of façades. On the few occasions that builders ever consulted workers they learned that their first priority was separate bedrooms for themselves and their children, even before privies.

'MODEL VILLAGES' IN BRITAIN

The French experiment with 'workers' cities' was largely sponsored by the state or municipal authorities. In Britain, private enterprise led the way for the first century of industrialisation, until Birmingham's radical mayor, Joseph Chamberlain, showed what civic effort could do in the 1870s. He swept away dank courts and replaced them with properly ser-

viced, decent dwellings. Until then, employers hoping to recruit workers for enterprises based in remote locations, like many mines and the early water-powered cotton mills, had little option but to provide them with accommodation. In 1768, Robert Morris had built Morriston to house Cornish copper miners. Richard Arkwright's Cromford, near Matlock in Derbyshire, was the first of the cotton factory villages. Built in the 1770s, it offered the workforce not only terraced houses but also shops, a church and a pub.

Later generations of employers came to appreciate that providing good housing helped to build a stable labour force. Establishing new industrial communities continued through the 19th century. In the North of England, Middlesbrough was founded in 1829 by a group of Quakers associated with the pioneering Stockton and Darlington railway. Intended as a coal-shipping port, it was laid out on a grid pattern. In 1831, its population was less than 200; by 1861, it was over 20000.

Bournville, laid out south of Birmingham by the Quaker chocolate manufacturer George Cadbury after 1879, provided its residents with generous gardens and became a model for suburban developers in the 20th century. Port Sunlight, south of Liverpool, was built from 1888 onwards to house employees of the Sunlight Soap factory. In 1913, it even acquired its own art gallery.

PULLMAN, USA

Most American company towns consisted of bleak board cottages and barracks with primitive sanitation. An exception was Pullman, built south of Chicago in 1879 by George M. Pullman, inventor of the luxury railroad sleeping car, to house his 2700 employees. Solid brick houses, in a style described as 'advanced secular Gothic', stood in neat rows, each home with its own front yard. The public facilities included an arcaded block of shops, a 1000 seat theatre, a 70 room hotel, a bank, a school, a fire brigade, a band, a free kindergarten and two parks. Company-sponsored clubs encouraged boating, ice-skating, cycling, baseball and, in deference to English immigrants on the payroll, cricket. The company also ran a gasworks, an ice plant, a dairy and a vegetable farm, fertilised with recycled sewage and dung from the communal stables.

AN IMPERIAL DIET FOR INDUSTRIAL WORKERS

WORLDWIDE COMMERCE and new methods of preserving food revolutionised the contents of the average British larder. Tea was grown in India from the 1860s and quickly replaced Chinese tea in the home market. The millionaire grocer Sir Thomas Lipton assured supplies for his shops by buying his own plantations in Ceylon. Sweetening was provided by sugar from the West Indies. Canada's vast prairies yielded wheat to cheapen the price of bread and thus enable the housewife to spend more on varying her family's diet. By the 1880s refrigerator ships were bringing beef, mutton, lamb and dairy produce from Australia and New

GLOBAL GROCER Thomas Lipton won a knighthood and a fortune by buying food in bulk and selling it to Britain's working class.

Zealand. Later came pineapples, bananas and other tropical fruits, chilled or canned. Less welcomed perhaps by many were sago and tapioca, detested staples of the nursery and boarding school. West Africa, however, provided compensation in the cocoa bean which, as a sweet, a drink and a flavouring, brought balm to the sweet-toothed British

and made stupendous fortunes for the Quaker Fry and Cadbury families, who saw it as a heaven-sent ally in the crusade for teetotalism.

Everything was spick and span – and there were abundant rules to keep it that way. The keeping of pigs or even chickens was forbidden. All repairs and gardening were done by contractors. Residents were bound by the terms of their lease not to enter their own homes with muddy boots.

By 1893, Pullman was valued at $8 million. That year, the town attracted many visitors who had come to Chicago to see the World Fair. It also saw many bank failures and a sudden and drastic fall in demand for railway rolling stock. George Pullman responded by slashing prices – and his men's

GARDEN SUBURB **Bedford Park in west London was laid out in the 1870s. Its spacious streets and villas proved attractive to artists and intellectuals.**

SPREADING THE WORD **Huge urban populations created new opportunities for advertising. The chemical industry was a leading spender, promoting the sale of soaps and patent medicines.**

wages – but not his managers' salaries, his shareholders' dividends or the rents he charged. The response was a strike in 1894, which cost 13 dead and 53 wounded before it was broken.

MEALS AND MEALTIMES – THE DINING CLASSES
In the model settlement of Mulhouse, married workers were strongly discouraged from using the communal restaurant on the grounds that 'the *pot-au-feu* is one of the cornerstones of the family and it would be irritating to see workers turn their backs on it in order to enjoy the pointless distrac-

BARE MINIMUM Bread and soup were staples in the diet of the French working class. By contrast, the table of a prosperous French family glitters with a profusion of crockery, glassware and silver. Ample, ritualised meals celebrated domestic solidity.

tions of a common table'. But as home and work-place became increasingly separated, and as ever larger numbers of children were sent to school, it became increasingly difficult for family members to eat together. In consequence, a major common meal on Sundays became important for all who could afford it. Among the more comfortable classes, it was usually eaten at midday, so that servants could have the afternoon off.

Meal times became more widely spaced as longer journey times added hours onto the working day. Breakfast in towns ceased to be a substantial meal, even among those who could afford it. The midday meal became less important when families were no longer able to gather together to eat it. The American millionaire and workaholic banker George Peabody took sandwiches to his office; most of his City of London competitors snatched a hasty meal in a 'chophouse', while their clerks patronised a kerbside coffee stall or a street seller of hot meat pies. Luncheon retained its importance, however, among the lower middle class who lived above their shops and workshops and in southern Europe, where it was followed by a siesta.

The main evening meal was eaten later and later. On the eve of the French Revolution in the 1780s, the fashionable classes dined between 4 and 5 pm. Half a century later, it was considered un-fashionably early to dine at 6. Guests were usually invited for 7.30 or 8, and it was considered polite to arrive five or ten minutes early. To fill the void between lunch and this later meal, the Duchess of Bedford in Britain made 4 pm the hour for tea, a meal which became so elaborated that by the 1870s Frenchman Hippolyte Taine likened it to an indoor picnic.

In 1861 the Englishwoman Mrs Isabella Beeton grandly pronounced in her *Book of Household Management* that: 'Dining is the privilege of civili-sation . . . The nation which knows how to dine has learned the leading lesson of progress.' Sophisti-cated dining required that the kitchens of the 'din-ing classes' themselves become increasingly more sophisticated. The smoky, open fires and spits of the 18th century gave way to cast-iron 'ranges' that incorporated ovens capable of baking or roasting at different temperatures, hot plates for boiling and a tank to supply constant hot water. In the hands of a skilled cook, who knew how to adjust its dampers to produce different temperatures in different places, the range represented a major advance on anything that had gone before; however, it required frequent 'blackleading' by the kitchen 'skivvy' to protect it from rusting – a messy and laborious task.

Storage cupboards, a well-ventilated larder with marble shelves and a stone or ceramic sink with a cold-water tap became standard even in the homes of the lower middle class. Gas cookers became available from the 1830s, but were not in common use until a generation later. There were hand-powered appliances for grinding, mincing and slicing as well as for making ice cream, stoning cherries and cleaning knife blades. By the 1890s, the most advanced kitchens had pressure-cookers and even electric kettles and toasters. Stone floors were covered by coir matting or linoleum.

FAST FOOD **A magazine cover of 1895 shows Parisians snatching breakfast at a street-side coffee stall on their way to work in the early morning.**

THE UNDERFED

While Mrs Beeton's middle-class readers learned how to dine in style, most Britons were still more preoccupied with the problem of nutritional survival. Advances in agriculture were slow to be re-flected in the diet of the poor. In Britain, many rural labourers virtually lived on 'tea-kettle broth' – a mess of stale bread softened with boiling water and flavoured with used tea leaves or scraps of onion or bacon. In France, bread accounted for half of the expenditure of the average poor family. The absence of food-storage facilities made preserved foods an important feature of the diet of the poor throughout Europe: salted fish in Portugal, smoked ham in Spain, sauerkraut and sausage in Germany, pickled onions and hard cheese in Britain.

To European observers the most remarkable features of the diet of the American working man were its plentifulness and the speed with which it was consumed. Europeans saw mealtimes as a valued interval for relaxation and conversation. Americans gobbled – in silence. Americans themselves acknowledged this national characteristic. In 1856, an article in *Harper's* on 'Why We Get Sick' noted that even the businessman rushes through his dinner 'where ten to one he is clinching a bar-

STEW QUEUE **German workers line up outside a factory kitchen in 1895. The bowls and spoons show that they are expecting broth or stew. Only a few employers realised that hot food could lead to greater productivity.**

SOLDIER'S PITY French cavalrymen distribute free soup outside their barracks. Wealthy race-goers in South Africa enjoy a lavish picnic, complete with champagne and silver cutlery.

gain . . . between bolted beef and bolted pudding'. The Americans' three daily meals were hugely generous in the size of their portions, even in boarding houses, but were virtually identical, consisting of meats and hot breads with few vegetables, despite their cheapness.

Works canteens were virtually unknown before World War I. Men took a cold snack with them to work. 'Cornish pasties' were originally eaten by tin-miners in Cornwall, who could grip the thick pastry edge with grimy hands, then throw it away; the most elaborate version had minced meat and vegetables baked in one end and a fruit filling at the other. In textile towns, where many married women worked, cookshops gave a much-needed service by roasting or stewing a main dish handed in by a wife on her way to work and picked up on her way home. Most working people ate hot food only in the evenings, and wives ensured that exhausted men came home to a solid meal, organising the rest of their working day around this pivotal point. In 1909, a major strike was sparked in the Welsh coalfield by a proposed change in the shift system which would have forced many women with husbands, sons and lodgers on different shifts to double the amount of time they had to spend preparing meals.

In matters of food, fathers were given preference in both quantity and quality. This was an acknowledgment that the well-being of the entire family rested on the health and stamina of the main breadwinner. As the person in charge of food preparation the wife often put her children next and herself last. Malnourishment was therefore most common among mothers and showed itself in loss of teeth and premature ageing.

Canned food, originally developed for military use during the Napoleonic Wars, became widely available towards the end of the 19th century. Tinned meat from Chicago, Cincinnati and Buenos Aires, canned fruit from Australia and South Africa began to feature on the tables of better-off working-class families, though the middle class remained suspicious. Condensed milk was much favoured by the urban poor in Britain as its high sugar content meant it could be kept longer than fresh cows' milk.

Printed warnings that condensed milk was unsuitable for infants were almost universally ignored – but at least showed that efforts were being made to educate the public in basic nutritional standards. This was an area of public policy in which Britain led the way, passing the first laws against food adulteration in 1860. For the inhabitants of large cities growing vegetables or even keeping chickens was often impossible. All food had to be bought. The deceptions practised on the unwary were gross and often positively harmful. Watering milk was most common and least injurious; it may even have been mildly beneficial as a large-scale survey of milk sold in London in the 1850s showed nearly every sample to have been contaminated with blood or pus. Other tricks included adding brick dust to pepper or cocoa, white sand to sugar and ground bones to flour and putting red lead in cheese to give it more colour.

MIND, BODY AND SPIRIT

Industry changed more than the world of work. It transformed societies and
unleashed new forces in fields such as schooling and politics. Workers formed
themselves into unions to defend their rights; rising levels of literacy brought
a thriving, mass-circulation press. The march of science was reflected in
astonishing discoveries that transformed the practice of medicine – from
anaesthetics to antiseptics to the improved control of such blights as cholera.

READING AND WRITING

The world of books had once belonged to the powerful and leisured. As political life was

opened to the masses and economic success came to depend on an ability to

acquire expanding arrays of skills, literacy became a necessity rather than a privilege.

INTELLECTUALS in the 18th century were confident of living in what came to be known as the 'age of Enlightenment' – but they were dubious about extending that happy state beyond their own ranks. It was by no means self-evident to them that education was a benefit for society as a whole, much less a universal human right. The Frenchman Voltaire, sworn enemy of superstition and ignorance, observed: 'It seems to me essential that there be ignorant wretches . . . We should preach virtue to the lowest class of people . . . When the populace meddles in reasoning, all is lost.'

In 1807, Davies Giddy, a future president of the British Royal Society, informed the House of Commons that 'giving education to the labouring classes . . . would . . . be found to be prejudicial to their morals and happiness; it would teach them to despise their lot in life, instead of making them good servants in agriculture, and other laborious

READ ALL ABOUT IT! Newspaper vendors outside the gates of a German factory. Mass-circulation newspapers developed attention-grabbing devices such as banner headlines and large pictures.

employments to which their rank in society had destined them; instead of teaching them subordination, it would render them fractious and refractory'.

Literacy was essential to members of the ancient professions – priests, lawyers and doctors – as the passport to the knowledge on which their power and prestige was based. Literacy, accompanied by numeracy, was essential for the bureaucrat, the merchant and the shopkeeper for their daily tasks.

But for the gentleman, literacy was an indicator of status, like the ability to fence or to ride stylishly. Learning, for many of the privileged, was another aspect of fine living, like elegant dress or a rich diet. To amass a library of 1500 books would cost the owner of a Virginia plantation as much as the 300 ton ship that carried his cotton to Liverpool. A hard-nosed mill owner in *North and South,* by the British novelist Mrs Gaskell, prides himself on having amassed a fortune through his native shrewdness and diligence – but still uses his leisure to compensate for a deficient education by learning Greek under the supervision of a local clergyman.

LEVELS OF LITERACY

But what did it mean to be educated? Of 754 recruits conscripted into the army of the German state of Mecklenburg-Schwerin in 1852, only 21 were totally illiterate, but 106 could only name letters, rather than read whole words, and 330 more could read only haltingly. A third could not write at all, and only a fifth could write well. More than half were quite unable to do simple sums.

Levels of literacy varied greatly between countries. Scotland had a higher literacy rate than England; the rural Netherlands outpaced industrialising Belgium, as Switzerland did Austria – three instances which imply that Calvinism, and a desire

---

DID YOU KNOW?

In 1833, the British Parliament voted £20 000 as its first grant for education and £50 000 for repairing the royal stables.

As late as 1863, 20 per cent of the population of France did not speak French but a provincial language such as Breton, Basque or Provençal.

NEW! IMPROVED! CHEAPER! Advertising on kiosks, buses and billboards – as in this Parisian street – assumed that more and more consumers were literate.

to be able to read the Bible, was far more important than commerce as a stimulus to learning. Literacy was highest in Sweden, where only 2 per cent of army recruits were illiterate by 1874, and lowest in Russia where, in the same decade, national literacy was only 21 per cent. America showed marked regional variations. By 1850, the South had more than 2700 private academies (more than the New England and Middle States added together), but the census of that year revealed that 20 per cent of Southern whites were illiterate against 3 per cent in the Middle States and a mere 1 per cent in New England. The arrival of uneducated European immigrants constantly depressed the overall national level of literacy, which was 17 per cent in 1880 and 11 per cent in 1900.

Industrialisation generated the wealth needed to build schools and pay teachers. But despite that, improved education for all classes came only slowly. As the British potter Charles Shaw put it as late as 1903: 'Only just now, after all these centuries, is the training of the millions beginning to be felt as a primal necessity . . . I began to work, but I could never see in what way my poor bit of education would prepare me for such as came to my hand. This began when I was a little over seven years of age. . . .'

SHHHHH!
Parents' concern for education spread even to the poor. An Italian immigrant (left) supervises his son's homework in the New York of the 1880s. And a French mother (above) sets an example of quiet concentration.

Economic and educational progress did not necessarily march hand in hand. In the early stages of industrialisation, standards of literacy may have actually fallen in textile and mining districts as children were sent to mills and pits as soon as they could earn. Industry created far less demand for literate workers than commerce did; a factory employing 1000 hands might have only two clerks.

In the long run, however, the need for a literate labour force provided a powerful motive for expanding educational opportunity. A correspondent of the British *Morning Chronicle* noted in 1849 a concern among London carpenters: 'The cause of the carpenters being so anxious about the education of their children lies in the fact that they themselves find the necessity of a knowledge of arithmetic, geometry and drawing in the different branches of their business.' In America, political and social considerations also played their part. In 1830 a meeting of Philadelphia working men resolved 'that there can be no real liberty without a wide diffusion of real intelligence; that the members of a republic should all be alike instructed in the nature and character of their equal rights and duties, as human beings, and as citizens . . . that until means of equal instruction shall be equally secured to all, liberty is but an unmeaning word, and equality an empty shadow'.

Others, though enthusiastic about certain aspects of education, were less keen on its liberating influences. The Englishwoman Hannah More, who established Sunday schools around the lead mines of the Mendip Hills in the first decade of the 19th century, reassured the Bishop of Bath and Wells: 'My plan of instruction is extremely simple and limited . . . I allow of no writing for the poor. My object is not to make fanatics, but to train up the lower classes in habits of industry and piety.'

SELF-HELP AND STATE HELP

The most common form of schooling provided in 18th-century England was the 'dame school', where village children were taught in a domestic parlour or the living room behind a shop. The teacher,

NO FOREIGN STUDIES

George Washington left money in his will to establish a national university. This would mean that Americans did not have to study abroad, where they might be contaminated by 'maxims not congenial with republicanism'. The money was never used. But the state of Georgia did pass an act barring any person educated abroad from public office for as many years as he had spent away.

A Schoolmaster's 'Ideal Home'

In 1881, the anticlerical government of Jules Ferry established a system of universal elementary education in France, aimed at combating the influence of the village priest over young minds. The schoolmaster became a missionary for secular enlightenment.

The ideal home for such teachers, which was sketched by Schools Inspector Richard, would establish a 'small sanctuary of order, industriousness and good taste'. The bed should be a plain iron frame, like those used by cadets at the Saint-Cyr military academy. The bathroom should have spotless white linen and be well enough equipped for its occupant to prove that he 'respects his person but eschews excessive sophistication'. The floor would be waxed to a shine, the straw-stuffed chairs kept free of all stains. Along the walls would be a selection of classic volumes, which, with a glass case for fossil or insect specimens, would serve as eloquent but silent testimony of an advanced education.

Green plants and a cage of songbirds would be permitted to soften the bachelor austerity. Another concession to luxury might be 'a magnificent table covering, made from an old shawl taken from his mother's wardrobe' – evidence of a comfortable background foregone. As the occupant advanced in his profession, he might add a piano, some 'casts of fine sculpture' and reproductions of masterpieces of European art 'brought within reach of every purse by the technique of photogravure'. In such a home, a teacher could receive pupils, parents and even the local *préfet* confident that it embodied the highest ideals of the Third Republic.

REPEAT AFTER ME Attentive Dutch children at a village school oblige the photographer with a model demonstration of disciplined obedience.

often a widow, occasionally a crippled man, struggled to impart the elements of basic literacy and the fundamental tenets of Christianity, usually without benefit of books, equipment or training and quite often with only the most minimal education to fall back on. A survivor of New Hampshire's early 19th-century school system recalled that it was 'the custom to employ those for teachers who were in the most need of support; if they could read a chapter in the Testament, teach the Shorter Catechism, and whip the boys, they were sufficiently qualified'.

In most cases, 'educational provision' may have amounted to little more than a child-minding service which allowed hard-pressed mothers to take on paid work. Nevertheless, the fact that many poor parents were prepared to part with even a few coppers to 'put the child to his letters' shows their eagerness to save their offspring from a life-sentence of illiterate poverty.

In the 1860s, the journalist Henry Mayhew was astonished to find that Eisenach, the capital of Thuringia in Germany, a 'city' with a population of 13 000, the size of a small English market town, supported a municipal kindergarten, which cared for 150 four to six-year-olds from 7 am to 7 pm – at

'THE HAPPY FAMILY' In well-off homes, childhood was idealised as a period of innocence to be protected.

a charge of one penny per year, including free bread and soup. The same town, apart from a variety of primary and secondary schools, also boasted a specialised forestry school, a seminary for training teachers and an exclusive ladies' academy with just 20 pupils, half of whom were English, 'mostly from Manchester'. Overall, he calculated that some 18 per cent of the local population at school age were receiving a regular education – compared to a national average of 12 per cent in Britain.

Most impressive was the systematic training given to these German teachers, which included mastery of the organ, violin and piano, so that they could all double up as director of music for a local

MECHANISED MEDIA   Printing the Illustrated London News by steam power in the 1840s. Printers were among the most literate section of the working class and in the forefront of the union movement.

**CITIZENS!
Printed posters offered a cheap method of communication between governments and the increasingly literate masses.**

church. In spite of that, their annual salary was equivalent only to 'the wages of an English dustman'.

In Britain, a major step forward came in 1822 with the foundation of the London Mechanics' Institute by Dr George Birkbeck. Essential back-up for its efforts came from the Society for the Diffusion of Useful Knowledge. Established in 1826, it concentrated on supplying what would now

be called 'distance learning materials' 'particularly to such as are unable to avail themselves of experienced teachers, or may prefer learning by themselves'. By 1850, there were over 700 Mechanics' Institutes in Britain.

Their target student was the craftsman who might possess a high level of practical skill, but had little understanding of the theoretical principles which governed his trade. Working shorter hours than the common labourer and less open to gross exploitation, he often had both the time and energy as well as the interest to attend 'night school'. He could also afford the modest fees charged for attendance. By supplying elementary instruction in mathematics and science, the institutes sought to bridge the gulf between theory and practice, and thus enable Britain to keep ahead of its emerging industrial rivals. Ironically, many working men showed less interest in 'practical subjects' than in literature, history or 'political economy', studies which conferred social cachet or assisted in the formation of self-confident working-class organisations.

A.G.G. Bonar, an English visitor to Switzerland around 1870, found the situation there far more to his liking: 'In the history of the Swiss working classes we have a significant view of the value of education, if not carried too far . . . While our artisans are wasting their time and money at a public house, the Swiss workman is busy with hand or brain preparing for the contingencies of the future . . . There are innumerable workingmen's associations which have some regular place of meeting, where books, periodicals, games and refreshments are provided for the members, whose time is chiefly engaged in debating, getting up dramatic performances and acquiring a knowledge of modern languages, book-keeping, drawing, arithmetic, history, etc.'

A Song for Europe? A French broadsheet of 1848 with the verses of a revolutionary battle hymn. The secret printing press became a powerful weapon of revolution.

The American equivalent of the Mechanics' Institute was the Lyceum, inspired by the writings of the English radical reformer, Lord Brougham. The first Lyceum was established in 1826 in Millbury, Massachusetts. Its main function was to offer courses of lectures on an apparently haphazard range of subjects. The institution was widely imitated, and by 1860 there were 3000 of them across the United States. In the 1870s they were reborn as 'Chautauquas', the first taking its name from a summer camp for Sunday school teachers at Lake Chautauqua, New York. The Chautauqua movement not only offered lectures, but soon supported them with correspondence courses. The itinerant lecturers for the Lyceums and Chautauquas were sometimes men of real distinction, such as the essayist Ralph Waldo Emerson, but there were also many rogues, who claimed to offer golden advice on what would later be called 'life-skills'. One delivered an exhortation on the keys to material success under the glittering title 'Acres of Diamonds'. It certainly served him well, as he gave the same address at least 6000 times.

As the right to vote was extended in many countries in the second half of the 19th century, and as trade competition sharpened between nations, so mass education became even more imperative on both political and economic grounds. Between the 1840s and 80s, Europe's population grew by 33 per cent – and school attendance by 145 per cent.

A REPUBLIC OF LETTERS

In America the struggle for free, tax-supported schools was fought out in the 1830s and 1840s. Despite opposition from those with vested interests against such schools – such as some private establishments – the principle of free education was

**Total Defeat of Bonaparte's
Principal Generals.**

Entrance of the Allies
INTO
PARIS.

FLIGHT *of the French* EMPRESS
And the KING *of* ROME.

*Proclamation in favour of the
House of Bourbon.*

ALL due thanks to the Almighty Disposer of
Events—we have this week the supreme happiness of congratulating our Readers upon a series of
Splendid Victories, the glorious heart-gladdening result of which is the Capture of the Capital of the
French Empire, which was entered by the Allied So-
vereigns, at the head of their Armies, on the 31st ult.
conformably to a Capitulation for that purpose, duly

EXTRA! EXTRA! An English
newspaper records a turning
point in the Napoleonic Wars
in 1814. In the American
South, a Mississippi paper
mingles local with national
news during the Civil War.

widely accepted by mid century; practical provision, however, came some decades later. In 1870
there were still only 160 public high schools in the
entire United States; by 1900 there were 6000.

New communities in America usually raised
their first school building by communal effort, with
parents paying the teacher a fixed amount per
child per month. Teachers, like rural preachers,
'boarded around', living with each family in turn,
for periods of not less than a week or more than a
month. In frontier Kentucky, teachers were paid
mostly in kind – venison, corn, homemade
whiskey, live pigs and even furs and bar-iron.

The typical one-room schoolhouse was often
less sanitary than the prisons of the day. The state
of Connecticut, which had used sales of 'reserve
land' in Ohio to finance its education system, was
accustomed to boasting that it had the best schools
in the country. If that was so, the national prospect
was dismal, for the average Connecticut schoolhouse was less than 20 ft long, 8 ft wide and 7 ft
high (6 × 2.4 × 2 m) – therefore rather smaller than a
railway freight car. Less than half had 'places of retirement' for either sex. There was a cast-iron stove
for heating, but no artificial lighting, and many had
windows 'glazed' with grease-proof paper. Poorer
children often paid their fees with firewood, while

those who were behind in paying were placed far-
thest from the stove.

As in Britain, few teachers were themselves well
educated and fewer still properly trained. Books
were dog-eared and rarely came in matching sets.
As pupils often varied widely in age and ability, this
may have mattered less than in a large school with
uniform classes, graded by age. Slates were universally used for 'ciphering' (arithmetic), with annual
production of these essential learning aids estimated
at 5 million as late as the 1890s. Learning depended
heavily on memorisation and recitation. The capitals
of the states of the Union were learned by singing
them to the tune of 'Yankee Doodle'. The widespread availability of *Webster's Speller* made spelling
synonymous with 'eddication' for many rural families, and the school spelling bee was a major cultural
event in the life of the community.

City schools in America were much better
equipped, with maps and globes and proper desks
and blackboards. By the 1870s, most had written
examinations to test the pupils and formal procedures for passing from one grade to the next.
Punctuality and regularity of attendance were more
strictly enforced. Teachers were better trained
than in rural areas.

Higher education expanded rapidly in America,
but most institutions were small and short-lived. As
early as 1800, the infant republic had 22 degree-
granting institutions – more than Britain and France
combined. By 1870, there were some 500 self-styled
colleges and universities, but they had only 5000 fac-
ulty and 50 000 students between them. Most professions, including the law, medicine and teaching
itself, could still be entered without a college diplo-
ma or even a high school education.

WHAT DID THEY READ?

In Britain, taxes on newspapers were introduced
in 1712 to restrict the free flow of information to
poorer people. The fears induced by the French
Revolution saw the stamp duty on a newspaper increased from 1½d in 1789 to 4d by 1815, bringing
the final cover price to 7d – a day's wage for an unskilled labourer.

Politically conscious people responded by club-
bing together to buy journals, which were passed on
from club members to workmates to neighbours to

AN ENGLISHMAN NOTES THE IGNORANCE OF HIS COUNTRYMEN

IN 1874, J.S. Stanley James, an Englishman, assisted Dr Edward Young, Chief of the US Bureau of Statistics, in compiling a survey of European labour conditions. In education, he found his countrymen to be disadvantaged, despite extraordinary examples of self-education:

❮ The English mechanic is the superior of other workers; but in education and social standing, how inferior to the American! His intelligence is mostly confined to his trade . . . Outside his trade he is too often ignorant of everything. A small proportion of mechanics may yearly become masters; now and then they become wealthy and enter ranks of the aristocracy or gentry. Then this ignorance of which I speak shows itself so plainly and makes the *nouveaux riches* of England notorious throughout the world. In this . . . I speak generally. I have seen a Manchester mechanic read Newton's *Principia* in the original. I know a London mechanic well read in . . . Greek who is learning Hebrew in order that he may study the Scriptures in that tongue. But the general ignorance of the workers of England arises from there not having been . . . any system of national education. The English mechanics I believe to be unsurpassed . . . but owing to that want of education . . . they are, outside their trades, far inferior to the American. ❯

CLIFFHANGERS IN MANHATTAN The US, where even children had disposable income, offered the first market for the cheap, illustrated 'comic book'.

friends. They were often read aloud for the benefit of the illiterate. As late as the 1850s, when 'taxes on knowledge' were being repealed, Henry Mayhew noted an avid appetite for information, even among street-traders: 'They are very fond of hearing anyone read aloud to them, and listen very attentively. One man often reads the Sunday paper of the beershop to them, and on a fine summer's evening a costermonger, or any neighbour who has the advantage of being a "schollard", reads aloud to them in the courts they inhabit.'

Sunday newspapers found a large market among the poor, for Sunday was, for most, their sole day of leisure. The *News of the World*, founded in 1843, had a circulation of 100 000 by 1854 but was outpaced by *Lloyd's Weekly News*, founded in 1842, which became the first British paper to pass the million mark, in 1896. Headlines from the mid-century local press indicate the topics with instant appeal: 'HORRIBLE MATRICIDE'; 'RAPE BY AN EX-LOVER'; 'THE MYSTERIOUS FRUITS OF SECRET LOVE'; 'FRIGHTFUL BOILER EXPLOSION'; 'MELANCHOLY DESTRUCTION OF A CHILD BY ITS MOTHER, WHILE FRANTIC WITH PAIN'.

The American press developed in similar fashion. The 200 newspapers of 1800 had become 1200 by the 1830s, when the *New York Sun* was launched as the first 'penny paper' and James Gordon Bennett began to exploit 'society' gossip and scandal to boost the sales of its rival, the *New York Herald*. Half a century later Joseph Pulitzer lifted newspaper rivalry to an entirely new level. When he bought the *New York World* in 1883 it had a circulation of 15 000. Fifteen years later it was more than a million. By the beginning of the 20th century, the United States had 2226 dailies – half the newspapers in the entire world.

SICKNESS AND HEALING

The 19th century saw some remarkable medical discoveries, such as the use of

anaesthetics and antiseptics. Even so, major improvements in health resulted

from better diets and a cleaner environment rather than more advanced medicine.

PEOPLE IN North America and Europe began to get healthier during the 18th century – not necessarily because doctors became more effective. It was more that some traditional curses, like malaria, declined in many regions. There were a number of reasons for this. Better agriculture meant more protein, which stiffened resistance to infection. At the same time, innovations in farming often brought other, unanticipated benefits.

The decline of malaria in northern Europe, for example, was almost certainly a side effect of the spread of turnip cultivation, which increased the supply of cattle feed and thus the size of herds. Mosquitoes were attracted to cows as larger, less irritable suppliers of blood than humans. As cows are not a suitable host for the malaria carried by mosquitoes, the chain of infection ended. Malaria was increasingly confined to Mediterranean areas, where summer droughts meant that cultivating root fodder-crops was less popular, and limited the size of cattle herds. In America, draining swamps diminished the breeding grounds of mosquitoes.

Another development was the expulsion of animals from human living quarters, which went

PATIENT PATIENTS Poor people in France queue for the attention of a physician. Many doctors worked part-time at charity clinics without pay.

A COUNTRY DOCTOR GAINS A REPUTATION

GUSTAVE FLAUBERT'S novel *Madame Bovary*, published in the 1850s, gave a vivid description of small-town life in provincial France. Here, a physician's success rested far more on the prominence of his various patients than on his own professional competence:

❝ Charles went upstairs to see the patient. He found him in bed, sweating under the clothes . . . a stout little man of 50 with fair skin and blue eyes, bald in front and wearing earrings. On a chair beside him stood a large flask of brandy, from which he helped himself at intervals, "to put some guts into him". When he saw the doctor, however, his spirits subsided and instead of swearing as he had been doing for the past 12 hours, he began to whimper.

The fracture was a simple one, with no complication of any kind. Charles could not have hoped for anything easier. Remembering his instructors' bedside manner, he comforted the injured man with a variety of bright remarks – the surgeon's blandishments, oil for his lancet, as it were. For splints, they fetched a bundle of laths from the cart shed. Charles selected one, cut it into sections and smoothed it down with a piece of broken glass, while the maidservant tore up some sheets for bandages. . . .

All went well: the patient made an exemplary recovery and when at the end of 46 days Rouault was seen attempting to walk round the yard unaided, Monsieur Bovary began to be considered a most capable man. . . .

One morning Monsieur Rouault came to pay Charles for setting his leg – 75 francs in 40 sou pieces, and a turkey. ❞

APPLIANCE OF SCIENCE A public disinfection team in England in 1877. Measures to improve public hygiene created a new market for the chemical industry.

ahead more quickly in, for example, England than France, with a corresponding fall in outbreaks of tuberculosis and brucellosis, which pass easily from animal to man.

HEALTH AND HOSPITALS

At the beginning of the 18th century, even the best physicians produced by famed medical schools such as Leyden in the Netherlands and Edinburgh still had no idea why most diseases occurred. They tended to regard illnesses as different symptoms of disorders of the entire body, to be dealt with by a generalised treatment such as a change of diet or bleeding, purging or sweating – all aiming to evacuate the body of impurities. Bleeding with leeches was the most common therapy, with enthusiasts drawing off up to four-fifths of the patient's blood supply. For small children already weakened by fever or dysentery, bleeding often proved fatal.

HEALTHY EATING Viennese consumers seek country-fresh farm produce. Foods processed in big cities were frequently adulterated.

CLINICAL CARE
White sheets and iron
bedsteads in a French
hospital of the 1880s.
Left: A female ward at
London's Middlesex
Hospital in 1808.

There were, however, forces that encouraged change. The expansion of maritime trade from the 15th century onwards had brought terrifying new diseases to Europe, jolting faith in time-honoured medical theories and provoking doctors to experiment. Repeated incursions of plague led to the eventual development of rigorous quarantine procedures in Mediterranean countries. At the same time, European patients were treated in hospitals as well as at home. Thus it became possible for doctors not only to observe different afflictions but to examine them constantly rather than periodically, while the patient was alive. They could also perform autopsies to enlarge their understanding of how death had occurred.

On the other hand, hospitals were also virulent sources of infection. Alfred Stillé, professor of medicine at the University of Pennsylvania, remembered the unmistakable smell which clung to the children's wing of the Philadelphia Hospital, where he studied as a young man in the 1830s: 'It is compounded of the exhalations of the habitually great unwashed; of effluvia generated by the decay of the sick, and the decomposition of their excretions; of the stale or rotting food that has been accumulated surreptitiously . . . from the heaps of musty old

boots and festering garments thrust out of sight and fermenting in unopened closets; and then, mingling with . . . all of these, a certain medicinal odor which may be traced to the accumulation of tinctures, and mixtures, and unguents, and plasters, upon the bedside tables of many patients.'

Ventilation was seldom adequate and overcrowding was often grotesque. A visitor to New York's Harlem Hospital as late as 1899 noted that many wards had between two and six patients laid out on canvas stretchers on the floor. Food was poor and prepared in insanitary, rat-ridden kitchens. Few

---

DID YOU KNOW?

France was the first country to require dentists to pass a professional examination before practising – in 1696. The United States followed suit in 1841 – and Britain in 1921.

A report of 1878 revealed that in the New Jersey State Asylum the standard procedure for detecting whether epilepsy was being faked was to spray the patient with alcohol and set fire to it. If the fit continued, it was genuine.

'A SUPPLIER OF MEDICAL NECESSITIES'

IT IS A CLOUDY NIGHT and therefore perfect. A man dressed in dark clothes nods slightly to the landlord as he leaves the Golden Boy pub. Outside, he pauses to throw a cloak around his shoulders. As if at a signal, a horse and cart clatter away noisily. The man strides briskly off in a different direction.

Two hours later, and miles away, they meet again, outside the padlocked gates of an iron-railed churchyard. Both the horse and the cart are now muffled by rags and, in the back of the cart, a woman crouches. At the turn of the lane, a boy lies hidden, but alert for passers-by. A duplicate key secures admission to the holy ground. (Sextons are poorly paid.)

Led by the woman, the man and the driver move towards a mound of newly turned earth, covered with wreaths and bouquets. The 'floral tributes' are removed systematically by the woman. As a grief-stricken 'relative', she made a note of their placing a few hours earlier. Meanwhile, the two men have spread a large tarpaulin on the ground. A third, burly figure appears from a clump of yew trees, clutching a pick and two spades. He and the driver dig fiercely until the coffin is reached.

Removing the coffin lid is quietly done, for it is noise, not damage, that matters. The corpse is hoisted to the surface with ropes and bundled into a sack. The burly man and the driver take it with them over the back wall of the cemetery. Outside is the boy, waiting with the cart. They drive away. The grave is filled in quickly but carefully, the surface soil reserved until last. The flowers are replaced.

Cautiously, the cloaked man and the woman leave and relock the gates. Tomorrow, he will return to the Golden Boy, and make for an upstairs room and

REST IN PEACE? Resurrectionists inspect a corpse as a magistrate and armed militia lurk in the background.

the briefest of meetings with a nervous medical student. They will drink briefly. Then, via back stairs, they will descend to a cool cellar, where, laid out on benches along the walls, his current 'stock' of young and old, male and female, will be on display. Both buyer and seller know that the corpses must be brought quickly to the dissecting table to be of use.

---

people had any sense of the importance of hygiene.

In the combat of skills versus ills, doctors depended almost entirely on their own five senses to identify a malady. Even in the late 19th century the 'snap diagnosis', based on swift observation of external symptoms, was still greatly admired. The first practicable stethoscope was not produced until 1819, nor the first clinical thermometer until 1866.

Training, too, often left much to be desired. A century after the United States' independence most of its medical men were still 'trained' by apprenticeship to a practitioner, usually for three years. As late as 1870, the head of Harvard Medical School admitted that it would be impossible to test students' proficiency with written examinations because most of the students 'cannot write well enough'. Many self-styled medical colleges were moneymaking businesses setting their own, usually dismal, standards.

ORDEAL BY SURGERY

In most circumstances, a patient contemplating surgery would have stood a much better chance of survival as a first-line infantryman at the Battle of Waterloo. Before 1832, British surgeons could only qualify by breaking the law. The supply of corpses legally available for dissection was far smaller than the demand. Medical schools therefore routinely bought the bodies of the newly dead, at two guineas a corpse, from 'resurrectionists', or body snatchers.

A law to increase the supply of legal corpses was passed in 1831 after an anatomy lecturer at King's College Hospital, London, denounced two men who tried to sell him the body of a 14-year-old boy whom he suspected, correctly, of dying of unnatural causes. The British Anatomy Act of 1832 ensured that corpses would be made available from the poorhouse and charity wards of hospitals, sparing the public the expense of many a pauper's funeral.

In the absence of anaesthetics other than alcohol or opium-based drugs, the best surgeons were those who cut fastest. Three minutes was reckoned a good time to amputate a leg. James Syme (1799-1870), recognised as the greatest surgeon of his day, took off the foot of Professor George Wilson at the ankle, rather than the knee, as most of his colleagues would have done. The operation, still known as 'Syme's amputation', caused less mutilation but prolonged the agony. Wilson was ambiguous in his gratitude: 'Of the agony it occasioned, I will say nothing. Suffering so great as I underwent cannot be expressed in words and . . . fortunately cannot be recalled. The particular pangs are now forgotten, but the black whirlwind of emotion, the horror of great darkness, the sense of desertion by God and man, bordering

close on despair, which swept through my mind and overwhelmed my heart, I can never forget however gladly I would do so.'

Without antiseptics, most patients undergoing major surgery died anyway. The introduction of anaesthetics from the 1840s – first ether, then chloroform, which was easier to administer – halved surgical fatalities, from two out of every three patients to one out of every three. Not only were patients spared the trauma of pain, but, because they were sedated and still, surgeons could work more slowly and accurately. Antiseptics, popularised by the Quaker Joseph Lister a generation later, improved the survival rate still further.

TREATING THE POOR

Treating oneself remained common, especially in rural areas where few formal medical services were available. Traditional herbal nostrums were passed on through generations, and not just among the poor. America proved a particularly fertile breeding ground for the experimental herbalist. Each immigrant group brought its own lore – from the Rhineland or Scottish Highlands or Ireland – and added it to the existing traditions of native Americans and the imported notions of African slaves. The woods of North America abounded in roots, barks and berries, which yielded numerous vile-tasting concoctions. Some were highly toxic, although useful in moderation Only after folk therapy had manifestly failed did one call on a doctor.

Increasing literacy proved a mixed blessing, as

SURE CURE FOR COSTIVENESS Fearing the expense of a visit to the doctor, many people were seduced by the extravagant claims of patent medicines.

DEADLY DIAGNOSES
A French cartoon mocks a
doctor fascinated by his
first encounter with a rare
disease. The 12-year-old
Ellen Hazard was the first
recorded English victim of
cholera in 1831. Even
when this scourge was
identified, doctors were
powerless to treat it.

body was also horrendous – severe
dehydration which wizened the skin
and turned it blue-black, rendering
plump, fair flesh and features hideous-
ly unrecognisable within hours.

What was even worse, no quarantine, however strict, seemed capable
of impeding its progress. The Bengal
outbreak of 1826 spread through
India, Persia, Russia, Poland and the
Baltic to reach the port of Sunderland
in north-eastern England in 1831. It then moved on,
via Ireland, to Canada and the United States, arriving in Mexico in 1833. In Britain, its legacy was
60 000 dead, and the establishment of the first official boards of health. A second visitation in 1848
led to a great strengthening of the boards' powers
and budgets, and an epoch-making investigation by
Dr John Snow, Queen Victoria's anaesthetist. He
turned medical detective to identify a single common water pump in Broad Street (now Broadwick
Street), Soho, London as the cause of infection for
some 500 local inhabitants. This proved that
cholera was spread by contaminated water.

Crusading 'sanitary reformers' pushed ahead
with the construction of modern drainage systems

it assisted the diffusion of both sound and spurious
information. The mid 19th century was a golden
age for the provider of patent medicines, which
could be advertised on posters or in the press without any check or control from the medical establishment. Claims for cure-alls were limited only by
their promoter's sense of the limits of public gullibil-
ity. 'Parr's Life Pills', for example, claimed to be
equally efficacious in curing both constipation and
diarrhoea. 'St Clair's Specific for Ladies' offered to
clear up both varicose veins and 'Tumurs' (sic).

Cholera terrified people into the beginnings of
sanitary self-defence. It was no more deadly than ty-
phus or typhoid, but it spread much more rapidly
and brought death more swiftly. The effect on the

DOCTORS OF DEATH

At least two American presidents were killed by
their physicians. George Washington was a fit 67
when he called in the doctors after catching a
bad cold; their bleeding, purges and poultices almost certainly finished him off. When President
Garfield was assassinated in 1881, the bullet was
retrieved by a surgeon whose unscrubbed hands
created the infection from which he died.

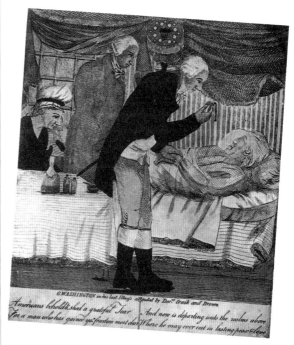

DEATHBED   The cold 'cures' administered to George
Washington probably did more harm than good.

THE CONQUEST OF SMALLPOX

SMALLPOX was the only major infectious killer that was identified and successfully dealt with in the 18th century. In 1721, Lady Mary Wortley Montagu, wife of Britain's Ambassador to Constantinople (Istanbul), brought news of a crude but effective procedure for inoculation practised in the Middle East.

This involved scratching the surface of the skin (usually between the thumb and forefinger) and introducing a small quantity of smallpox pus under the skin, thus deliberately giving the person a limited dose of the infection – as a result of which they developed an immunity to the full-blown disease. The only equipment needed was a needle to make the prick with, and a nutshell to carry the pus in.

Lady Mary had herself survived smallpox at the age of 26 – but was disfigured for life. In 1718, she had therefore had her six-year-old son inoculated. In London, a trial of the Turkish technique was made on six criminals awaiting the rope. All survived. Reassured by these clinical trials, the royal family had their children inoculated in 1722.

By the 1740s, travelling inoculators were doing a steady trade in small English towns and villages, though there was little interest in the big cities, where smallpox was just one more disease among many. In 1768, Catherine the Great

COUNTRY DOCTOR Edward Jenner, pioneer of vaccination, preferred his native Gloucestershire to fame and fortune in London.

of Russia imported an English doctor to immunise herself and the Crown Prince – but stopped at that. In 1774 Louis XV of France died

from smallpox; seeing the fate of his brother king, Frederick II of Prussia hastily ordered an inoculation programme in his domains. One of George Washington's first military decisions in 1776 was to order the inoculation of his army.

In 1798, an English country doctor, Edward Jenner, published a pamphlet outlining his experiments to produce immunisation against smallpox by inoculating patients with cowpox, a less virulent infection. This safer procedure was known as vaccination, from the Latin for cow – *vacca*. Within five years, it was being practised as far away as Mexico and Kentucky; within seven in the Philippines and on the Russo-Chinese border.

PAMPHLET POWER Pamphlets preached the virtues of vaccination.

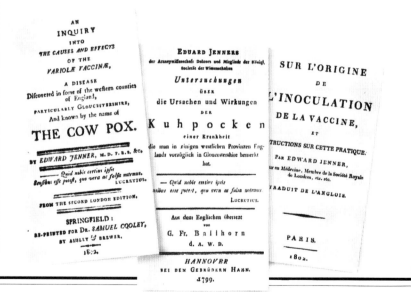

which used steam power to flush sewage through ceramic pipes at regular intervals, rather than leaving it to accumulate in brick caverns until it spilled over into rivers and streams from which the poor still drew their water for drinking and cooking. New York followed London's example after 1866, Hamburg not until 1892, the year before a cholera vaccine was at last developed. Providing efficient

sewage disposal and clean water supplies diminished the threat, not only of cholera but of other waterborne diseases, such as typhoid.

Cholera was spectacular, but in sheer numbers tuberculosis was far more deadly. 'Consumption' was Europe's biggest killer and afflicted an estimated seven out of ten of its population, although only about one in seven died of it. The most vulnerable

FLUSHED WITH PRIDE Parisian sightseers inspect the wonders of their city's sewerage system in 1870. The sewer workers wear protective clothing.

were industrial workers, recent immigrants and the homeless. The damp, overcrowded, jerrybuilt cities of the 1820s and 30s, where the atmosphere was laden with coal dust, cotton fibres, sulphur and lead, provided TB with an ideal environment. In the 1840s, it accounted for half of all the deaths in a Berlin orphanage.

Middle-class sufferers usually recovered following rest, attentive nursing, adequate diet and clean, airy surroundings. Better food and housing, meanwhile, along with less destructive working conditions and cities made healthier by parks and squares, led consumption to abate of its own

accord, even before the German pathologist Robert Koch finally identified the tubercle bacillus swimming under the lens of his microscope in 1882.

NATIONAL HEALTH, NATIONAL STRENGTH

In 1805, Napoleon ordered his troops to be vaccinated against smallpox. Other military campaigns spurred on improvements that later benefited civilians. The Crimean War elevated Florence Nightingale to a national heroine in Britain, and gave her the influence and means to raise nursing to a semisacred 'vocation'.

As international tension rose towards the close of the 19th century, governments' concern for the health of recruits mounted with it. Detailed analysis of the physical condition of British volunteers for service in the Boer War (1899-1902) led to the appalling conclusion that, of this sample of the nation's youth, only two out of every nine were fully fit for combat. The publication of these results in 1904 was soon followed by the introduction of school medical inspections and free school meals.

INFERNAL ATMOSPHERE Long hours in nauseous environments, like this French gasworks, shortened many lives with lethal respiratory diseases.

SOCIETY'S BUILDING BLOCKS

The Industrial Revolution both divided nations and united them. On the one hand,

it created new extremes of wealth and poverty. On the other, inequalities that

had once been accepted as a law of nature were challenged as injustices to be remedied.

FROM THE END of the 18th century the notion that classes formed the building blocks of society began to overtake traditional concepts such as 'rank', 'order', 'estate' or 'degree'. People were more and more aware that social positions were the outcome of human arrangements, rather than divine law, and could therefore be made rather than simply inherited. With the coming of industry, they began to realise that they could make fortunes or, equally quickly, be reduced to poverty. Social divisions could be challenged and changed.

At the time the United States' Constitution was framed, James Madison argued that moneyed and manufacturing interests 'grow up of necessity in civilised nations and divide them into different classes, actuated by different sentiments and views'. That was one of the earliest recorded uses of the word 'class' in something like its modern sense. By 1831, Britain had a (short-lived) 'National Union of the Working Classes', which identified its enemy as 'property or capital'. Similar attitudes gave rise to the revolutionary French epigram 'property is theft'.

SO NEAR, SO FAR Life in cities tantalised the destitute with visions of other people's security and comfort.

WORKERS UNITE

Another slogan, 'Unity is strength', would become a commonplace of trade union rhetoric, but to turn it into action took time. As the English slum-dweller Robert Roberts observed, his working-class neighbours in Salford, far from being 'united by a common aim and culture', were constantly staking their claims to varying levels of 'respectability' through such outward signs as a line of unpatched washing or a gleaming front doorstep. At the top end of Roberts' world stood publicans, small shopkeepers and the skilled 'aristocracy of labour', who,

AWARENESS AND APATHY DIVIDE 'THE WORKING CLASS'

THE JOURNALIST Henry Mayhew was struck by the different approaches to politics of London artisans and labourers in the 1850s:

❦ In passing from the skilled operative of the West End to the unskilled workman of the e a s t e r n quarter of London, the moral and intellectual change is so great that it seems as if we were . . . among another race. The artisans are almost to a man red-hot politicians . . . It is true that they may entertain exaggerated notions of their natural rank and position in the social scale, but at least they have read and reflected . . . The political character and sentiments of the working classes appear to me to be a distinctive feature of the age, and they are a necessary consequence of the dawning intelligence of the mass . . . That they express their opinions violently, and often savagely, it is my duty to acknowledge; but that they are the unenlightened and unthinking body of people . . . it is my duty, also, to deny. . . .

The unskilled labourers are a different class of people. As yet they are as unpolitical as footmen. Instead of entertaining violently democratic opinions, they appear to have no political opinions whatever; or, if they do possess any, they rather lean towards the maintenance 'of things as they are', than towards the ascendancy of the working people. ❦

through education and attendance at chapel, encouraged their offspring to rise into the lower middle class – the most rapidly growing social group – as clerks or teachers. At the bottom of the heap came casual labourers and street sellers and, below them, workhouse paupers, who 'hardly registered as human beings at all'.

In Britain would-be labour organisers also faced the hostility of the Combination Acts, passed at the height of the French Revolutionary Wars in 1799 and 1800, which defined unions as criminal conspiracies. Some attempted to function under the guise of 'friendly societies' – do-it-yourself social security clubs which were permitted by law. Others went underground, administering oaths to new recruits and bolstering internal discipline with bloodcurdling threats of the consequences of betrayal. Most early labour unrest, however, was not organised by unions at all but took the form of spontaneous riots, machine-smashing and arson. The repeal of the Combination Acts in 1825 opened the way for legitimate activity, much of which was diverted into overambitious schemes to unite all members of one trade, or even all trades. Many of these projects overlapped with political movements.

One movement was Chartism, which had a programme for the reform of Parliament in the six points of the 1838 'People's Charter' – universal male suffrage, secret ballots, equal electoral districts, annual elections, the abolition of property

YOU'RE THE BOSS A straw-hatted French foreman poses confidently beside cloth-capped labourers. White-collared clerks in a London office (below) are arranged in a complex hierarchy.

CRUCIBLE OF 'CLASS' A US ironworks around 1865. Most employers resisted the forming of workers' unions.

A BATTALION COMMANDER IN THE ARMY OF LABOUR

NOWADAYS George Oldroyd wears a watch and chain with seals and has a clean collar every other day. But he still has the hands and voice of a working man. As one of the new breed of permanent, paid union officials, he is a man of consequence.

George's wife serves his breakfast. As his evenings are usually taken up with meetings, the first hour of the day is their best chance to talk. With a son in Canada, another at sea, a daughter in service and the youngest dead from diphtheria they are effectively childless. George listens to Martha's shrewd daily review of local gossip and rumour. His members – he thinks of them as 'his' men – are much like him, skilled, solid, married and moderate. Their wives know the price of everything and expect their husbands to know the value of their labour. If Martha tells him that the corner shops are refusing 'tick', he knows that he will soon hear grumbling and whispers. He gained his position by seeing trouble before it arrives. He has a few hotheads in his branch, who think a strike the answer to every problem. George knows that strikes work when trade is good, not bad; then employers fear a hold-up – and can pay up.

At his one-room office George scans the newspaper. There is nothing worth following up. His correspondence is a letter from central office, summoning him to a meeting next month. He spends the rest of the morning with his bookkeeper, a one-time boiler-maker who can still write a fair copperplate with his remaining hand.

At noon George visits an engineering works. As the town's largest employer it merits a fortnightly call. George talks with three or four of his members as they munch their 'snap' and sup cold tea. The chat is casual – cricket and pigeons and gardens – but he remains alert for more serious matters.

On the way back across town, George stops at the Infirmary where one of his men is 'on the sick'. It is not serious and he will soon be back paying his 'subs' rather than drawing on the branch's slender welfare funds. George spends the rest of the afternoon gathering his papers and his thoughts for the evening's meeting, when he will support the efforts of a new organiser to start up a branch in the next town.

ARTISAN ARISTOCRACY A certificate issued by Britain's Amalgamated Society of Engineers celebrates its members' craft skills.

KNOWING YOUR PLACE
Traditionalists gave each class a characteristic virtue. The wealthy (left) exhibited leadership, the middle class (far left) sought respectability and the poor (below) were expected to show deference.

qualifications for candidates and the payment of MPs. Abortive armed Chartist 'risings' in areas as different as rural Wales and highly industrialised Lancashire unnerved the government enough to make it police disaffected areas with the army. In 1848 a quarter of a million people assembled south of the Thames in London to present a petition to Parliament. The Duke of Wellington was appointed to coordinate the defence of London and thousands of special constables were sworn in.

In the event, it rained and, without any well-organised leadership, the crowd dispersed peacefully. As the economy picked up, Chartism declined. Three years later the railways were bringing millions to London, not to overawe Parliament, but to gawp at the wonders of the Great Exhibition.

HOME, SWEET – SECURITY
An advertisement for a building society in Edwardian Britain plays on the ambition to own one's home.

In Britain, effective unions date from the mid 19th century, with the establishment of bodies such as the Amalgamated Society of Engineers. Migrants also carried the lessons of British experience to places such as Australia, where the economic boom of the 1870s favoured a strong labour movement. By 1876 the Sydney and Melbourne seamen's unions had merged to create the Federated Seamen's Union of Australia. Three years later an Intercolonial Trade Union Congress was held in Sydney. In 1889, the Australian labour movement demonstrated its power by an imaginative gesture – sending £30 000 to support London dockers in their struggle for a minimum 6d an hour ('the docker's tanner') – thus enabling the Londoners to win a famous victory.

In continental Europe, the development of unions in places like Germany was held back by political reaction after the failed liberal revolutions of 1848-9. Although the right to strike was legalised in 1872, German society was dominated by the military and its cult of obedience and the pace of forming unions remained slow. The most advanced, factory-based sector of

CONFRONTATION AND CELEBRATION Chartists gather to deliver a monster petition to the British Parliament. It rained and they all went home. An exuberant German composition commemorates 50 years of industrial success for the Heckmann foundry.

first decade of the 20th century, only about a fifth of the industrial labour force was unionised.

In the United States, the working men's organisations campaigned for large general aims rather than specific industrial objectives. They identified banks, monopolies and large corporations as their enemies and placed great faith in free, tax-supported schools as a panacea for many ills.

FRONTIERS OF FAITH
Radical politics often went hand in hand with anti-clericalism; even so, religion continued to appeal to many people in all classes. In the United States,

the economy, which elsewhere provided the vanguard of unionism, was held back by the paternalism of the giant manufacturers of armaments and chemicals as well as by state welfare measures, such as provisions to insure workers against sickness, deliberately introduced in the 1880s to pre-empt working-class unrest. By the

LEFT, LEFT, LEFT French socialists march in support of strikers under the watchful eye of mounted gendarmes in 1896.

where the Constitution explicitly separated Church and state, the religious life displayed a vigour that provoked wonder in visiting Europeans. By the end of the 19th century, there were over 150 denominations and sects to choose from. On the frontier, itinerant preachers carried the Bible and news of the wider world to thousands of embryonic settlements and isolated farmsteads. Americans accommodated self-sustaining communities of religious refugees from Europe, such as the Moravians, Shakers, Amish, Mennonites and Hutterites. They even spawned entirely new faiths, such as Mormonism, Seventh-Day Adventism, the Jehovah's Witnesses and Christian Science.

The prestige of the clergy, especially in educated communities, was high although they were usually poorly paid. In small, and especially new, towns clergymen played a crucial role as leaders, serving indefatigably on committees, organising and fund-raising for schools and charities. In the emerging big cities, however, the established Churches lost ground, as they did in Europe. In the 1880s it was estimated that 60 000 people in central Chicago had no church of any kind available to them. Instead, it was the flamboyant revivalists and novel initiatives, such as the YMCA and the Salvation Army, both introduced from Britain, that made the most impact on the deprived and dislocated inhabitants of the big cities.

In Britain, a deep Christian conviction inspired the lives of many of the greatest heroes of the age: the explorer-missionary David Livingstone; the nursing pioneer Florence Nightingale; the soldier General Gordon; and Lord Shaftesbury, the aristocratic philanthropist. Regular church attendance was an essential badge of respectability. Nevertheless, in 1851, when a census of church attendance was taken in Britain, the nation was shocked to discover that two-thirds of the population had not been involved in any form of religious worship.

In working-class areas, Methodist and other sectarian chapels almost always had Sunday schools attached to them. These had a

DID YOU KNOW?

When a team of British and American scholars produced a revised version of the King James Bible in the 1880s, 200 000 copies of the New Testament were sold in a single week in New York alone, and both of Chicago's major newspapers printed the text in its entirety.

In Britain in 1870, 200 000 people with incomes of £300 or more a year were liable to pay income tax. The tax payable on £300 would be £5.

US department store tycoon Marshall Field (1834-1906) earned $600 an hour – more than one of his counter-assistants would earn in three years.

vital role in providing supplementary education for children and remedial education for adults. Many men graduated from learning their letters from the Bible, to preaching in the pulpit, to addressing a meeting of fellow trade unionists. In Britain, at least, socialism and the trade union movement owed far more to Methodism than to Marxism.

THE CHURCH UNDER CHALLENGE

By 1914 far fewer Europeans professed themselves Christians than a century before. This may have been partly due to the progress of medicine. Infant deaths were less common; anaesthetics diminished

SHOW ME THE LIGHT
A US city mission hall with gas lighting for evening meetings. 'Missions' sought to remedy the shortcomings of the established Churches.

TAKING RELIGION TO THE INNER CITIES

IN 1860 Dwight L. Moody gave up his job as a shoe salesman to sell salvation, working with the Chicago YMCA, founding his own church and conducting missions in the slums. With the hymn writer Ira D. Sankey, a fine tenor, he promoted the 'gospel hymn' and made high-profile extended tours of Britain in 1873-5 and 1881-4. In the United States, he and Sankey brought religion to the cities – so successfully that their visits brought a downturn in theatre takings. Moody's preaching was sensational but straightforward – the Bible was literally true and the Second Coming imminent. With the full force of his 20 stone (127 kg) frame, he bellowed out his demand for belief.

He had no time for sectarian subtleties, even less for Darwinism. His mass revivals were generously funded by sympathetic business contacts. Moody himself was generous to charities, but he also believed that the divine regeneration of the individual was the only real way to solve society's deepest problems. His memorials are a seminary for girls and the Moody Bible Institute in Chicago.

PIED PIPER OF CHICAGO
Moody's adoring Bible class of 'guttersnipes' eagerly provided him with a street escort.

suffering; and antiseptics reduced the risks of infection. If the afflictions of mortality and disease still forced men and women to their knees, many did so less often. As a result, the Churches began to compete for custom. In Catholic countries, the parish churches sponsored Mother's Unions to ensure that the rising generation adhered to the faith of their ancestors, and savings banks to help the provident to ride out the rough seas of unexpected unemployment or sudden sickness.

Unquestioning belief was further undermined by advances in scholarship. Few slum-dwellers had heard of Charles Darwin and his unsettling ideas about how humankind had evolved. But editors of newspapers, trainers of teachers and members of town councils had heard such things, in however muddled a way. In the past such people had set an example of certainty. Now they were less sure.

On the other hand, mass travel revitalised the pilgrimage. The English pioneer of the package holiday, Thomas Cook, himself a Baptist preacher, was quick to grasp the marketing potential of following 'in the footsteps of St Paul' and had tours to the Holy Land by the 1870s. Railway travel also revived a number of traditional centres of Catholic devotion. Assisi proved a magnet to Catholics and Protestants alike. Visions, usually by children, created further new centres of mass devotion at La Salette (1846) and Lourdes (1853) in France, Ilaca (1865) in Croatia, Philippsdorf (1871) in Bohemia and Knock (1879) in Ireland. Each of these revelations was initially greeted with clerical caution and agnostic mockery; both reactions were swept aside by the torrent of popular acclaim.

DOORSTEP SALVATION Salvation Army 'slum sisters' lived in pairs in deprived areas of British cities where they preached temperance, hygiene and the gospel.

LIFE IN THE CITY

In 1800 there were 65 cities in the world with more than 100 000 inhabitants; by
1850 there were 106. In the 1850s, only London, Paris and New York had a
population of over 1 million; 16 cities did by 1900. Railways, newspapers and
advertising combined to spread urban influences into the countryside. At the
same time, a new world needed new kinds of entertainment. Competitive sports,
from football to baseball, were codified; music halls and theatres flourished.

SURVIVAL IN THE CITY

The cities of the industrial era often seemed to be out of control, defying efforts to

limit their growth or cope with the consequences of growth. Efficient policing,

public hygiene and transport lagged behind the need for them.

VISITORS TO England's cotton-manufacturing capital Manchester – 'Cottonopolis' as it became known – were torn between awe and despair. The preacher Sydney Smith dismissed it as 'a horrid unfinished town'; the poet Robert Southey believed that 'a place more destitute of all interesting objects than Manchester it is not easy to conceive'. Its famous factories reminded him of 'convents, without their antiquity, without their

beauty, without their holiness . . . where when the bell rings it is to call wretches to their work instead of to their prayers'.

The Frenchman Alexis de Tocqueville visited Manchester in 1835 and was overwhelmed by the fug, reek and din of the world's newest urban midden, an environment utterly alien to his experience: 'A sort of black smoke covers the city. The Sun seen through it is a disc without rays. Under this half daylight 300 000 human beings are ceaselessly at work. A thousand noises disturb this dark, damp labyrinth but they are not at all the ordinary sounds one hears in great cities. The footsteps of a

PALL OF THE CITY Smoke belches from factories in the Saar region on the French-German border. Pollution spread out into the surrounding countryside.

WAR ON FILTH Dustmen on their rounds in London's East End around 1890. Improved public hygiene had become a priority with city authorities.

busy crowd, the crunching wheels of machinery, the shriek of steam from boilers, the regular beat of the looms, the heavy rumble of carts, those are the noises from which you can never escape in the sombre half-light of these streets.' Missing were the sounds and sights a culti-vated Frenchman thought of as the essence of sophis-ticated city life: 'The clatter of hoofs as the rich man drives back home . . . the gay shouts of people amusing themselves . . . music heralding a holiday . . . smart folk strolling at leisure in the streets.'

But, as de Tocqueville also realised, Manchester was a potent symbol of a new era in the history of the planet. In its own terms, the city was a roaring success. Karl Marx's collaborator, Friedrich Engels, whose father was a mill-owner, ruefully recorded a characteristic example of Mancunian self-confidence: 'I once went to Manchester with a bourgeois, and spoke to him of the bad, unwhole-some method of building, the frightful condition of the working people's quarters and asserted that I had never seen so ill-built a city. The man listened quietly to the end, and said at the corner where we parted: "And yet there is a great deal of money made here. Good morning, sir".'

Manchester inspired Marx and Engels with the vision of a cataclysmic future that runs through the

EYEWITNESS

CLUBBING TOGETHER – A SAVING VIRTUE

A SURVEY of working-class life by the British *Morning Chronicle* in 1849-51 found that 'the principle of association for mutual benefit' amounted to a virtual mania in the Birmingham area:

❧ Even infants of two or three years of age are taught to club their half-pence, for medical attendance, or for the purchase of Sunday finery. Any one who walks along the streets, and looks at the placards on the walls, or the bills in public houses, coffee-houses and other shop windows, may see at a glance from these announcements how deep a hold the club system has taken upon the affections of the people . . . The father of the family clubs for his Trade Society, or for the Odd Fellows, or for a Sick and Burial Society, or for a Money Club, or for a Watch and Seals Club, or for an Excursion Club. The mother joins a Medical Attendance Club, or a Coal and Coke Club, or a Flour Club, or a Shawl Club, or a Silk Dress Club, or, at Christmas time, a Pudding Club . . . while the children, if at school, bring their fortnightly halfpence to a Sick Club, or a Clothing Club; or, if at work in a factory, contribute at a specified rate to the club of the establish-ment . . . One of the newest clubs of working men in Birmingham has been constituted . . . [to enable its] members to visit the Great Exhibi-tion of the present year. ❧

FAREWELL ARCADIA As late as 1874 Pittsburgh (top) retained a clearly rural setting. By 1890, the streets of Chicago (above) were overshadowed by high buildings, creating an environment that was unmistakably urban.

pages of the *Communist Manifesto*, first published in 1848. By then, however, Manchester had embarked on a campaign of civic salvation. Three public parks were opened in 1846, and the water supply system was extended in 1847. In 1856, the 'Free Trade Hall' was opened, its name proclaiming the city's fundamental economic philosophy – unrestricted trade across the world, without barriers imposed by protective tariffs and the like. The hall soon became best known as the home of a great symphony orchestra, the creation of musical director Charles Hallé. And in 1877 an imposing Town Hall was completed at the cost of around £1 million, its Great Hall adorned with murals depicting episodes in the city's rise to eminence. Half a century after de Tocqueville's visit, Manchester had acquired the trappings of civic culture.

THE SHOCK OF THE NEW – AMERICA

Manchester grew mightily with the early industrial age, thanks largely to the crisscrossing rivers that supplied power to the first generation of textile machines and then water for the boilers of the steam-powered ones that displaced them, but as a settlement it dated back to Roman times. Other cities sprang almost literally from nowhere. Of these, Chicago in the United States saw the most dramatic transformation. In 1830, it had a population of about 50 and considerably more pigs than houses. By 1890 it had a population of more than a million and was the second city of the Americas.

Chicago owed its growth to its position rather than its resources. Its harbour provided a welcome refuge from the storms of Lake Michigan, and it stood at one end of the shortest route from the Great Lakes to the Mississippi. By 1852, it was connected to New York by rail, and only four years later, it was the hub of a network of ten lines, tentacles of commerce that penetrated deep into the newly settled and increasingly productive farmlands of United States' Midwest. It was claimed that the hogs processed in the city each year would, if they were placed nose to tail, reach all the way to New York. By 1870 the city's grain elevators were handling 60 million bushels (75 million cu ft – 2 million m³) annually, and the lumberyards were selling 1.5 billion ft (455 million m) of timber.

After a fire in 1871 had devastated the city, the authorities embarked on an ambitious scheme of linked parks and boulevards. The boulevards, from 200 to 400 ft (60 to 120 m) wide, had a central drive for carriages and parallel bridleways for people on horseback; in 1881, it was reported that no fewer than 4700 carriages had been counted going south on Grand Boulevard on a single Sunday afternoon.

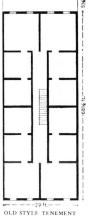

OLD STYLE TENEMENT

BUILDING BETTER BARRACKS
Some New York tenements had handsome façades. Two sets of plans show the effects of tighter building regulations. By the 1880s, new tenements (on the right) had to have windows even in the inner rooms.

119

In the decade of its reconstruction, Chicago took full advantage of its pivotal position in the nation's transport system to become the home of the world's first major mail-order firm, Montgomery Ward & Co; by 1876 its catalogue carried 3899 items, from tombstones to baby clothes.

James Bryce, a future British Ambassador to Washington, thought that the Chicago of the 1880s was 'perhaps the most typically American place in America'. That was a very diplomatic judgment. Most British visitors disliked it. Matthew Arnold thought it 'a great uninteresting place', Robert Louis Stevenson found it 'great and gloomy', and Kipling hated it: 'Having seen it, I urgently desire never to see it again. It is inhabited by savages . . . its air is dirt.' On the other hand, the American writer Mark Twain found Chicago exhilarating and warned: 'It is hopeless for the occasional visitor to try to keep up with Chicago – she outgrows his prophecies faster than he can make them.'

Chicago's dynamism was characteristic of the whole of the Midwest in the 1880s. Detroit, Milwaukee, Columbus and Cleveland all grew by 60 to 80 per cent. In 1890, the year in which the Federal Bureau of the Census finally pronounced the American frontier 'closed', 12 of America's 50 largest cities were in the Midwest – a striking contrast to the beginning of the century when the only

major cities were 'waterfront' settlements such as New York, Boston, Philadelphia, Baltimore, Charleston and New Orleans.

Chicago was also typical in its ethnic mixture. Although Scandinavian immigrants generally preferred the farm to the city, there were 70 000 of them working in Chicago by 1890, the men butchering hogs or assembling McCormick reapers, and the women mastering English as domestic servants. They were outnumbered by the Germans, who were prominent in skilled trades such as locksmithing, lithography, photography and tailoring. The Germans, in their turn, were outnumbered by the Irish and by the new arrivals from southern and eastern Europe, the Italians and Jews from Poland and Russia. As a result, the foreign-born population of the Chicago of 1890 outnumbered the entire Chicago population of 1880. One commentator pointed out that only two German cities had more Germans than Chicago; only

NIGHT REFUGE 'Improvement' schemes, as in Paris (above), destroyed slums without necessarily rehousing those displaced. This forced them to seek shelter in 'night refuges' such as this German one (right).

that there would be an enormous hidden profit outweighing any loss . . . the Woolworth Building was going to be like a giant signboard to advertise around the world his spreading chain of five-and-ten-cent stores'.

THE CENTURY OF THE CITY

Most European cities, such as Essen, Lille, Prague and Marseilles, grew from an ancient core, though this did not necessarily mean that the core itself grew. For example, the population of the City of London, the capital's oldest part, declined by more than two-thirds over the course of the 19th century.

The spread of the city was often eased by the demolition of ancient bonds. London lost its city gates in the 18th century; Brussels and Antwerp razed their fortifications in the 19th. In Vienna the city walls were pulled down in 1857 to make way for wide boulevards that swung in a circle round the medieval city. The resulting Ringstrasse, opened in 1865, was 60 yd (55 m) wide and more than 2 miles (3.2 km) long, lined with trees and illuminated with gas burners. During the following quarter century, it provided a stately setting for a series of major public buildings in a medley of architectural styles – a neo-Renaissance opera house and university, a Gothic town hall and a classical parliament.

Vienna grew eightfold during the 19th century,

two Swedish cities had more Swedes, and only two Norwegian ones had more Norwegians. The new arrivals tended to huddle together, islands of neigh-bourliness in an ocean of indifference or hostility. With their panoply of ethnic shops and foreign-language newspapers, the score of different com-munities proved so self-sufficient that many chil-dren grew up more like second-generation immi-grants than first-generation Americans.

Chicago was also the birthplace of the skyscraper. In 1891 Maitland's *American Standard Dictionary* became the first known dictionary to include the word, defining it as 'a very tall building such as are now being built in Chicago'. Steel-framed, with internal communications revolutionised by the safety elevator and the recently invented tele-phone, they were modest by later standards, aver-aging 12 to 16 storeys. New York, where office rentals were four times as high, soon overtook Chicago's pioneering efforts, spurning the stripped-down, economical 'Chicago style' in favour of fan-tastical spires, domes and columns.

The results were distinctive. When the contrac-tor for the 1911 Woolworth Building confessed his dismay that it would never realise an economic return, 'Mr Woolworth let me into his secret –

becoming many times larger than its nearest national rival. Brussels, Berlin, Madrid, Warsaw, Copenhagen and Stockholm all achieved similar feats in their respective countries. But the city that grew most spectacularly was Budapest, which was 16 times larger in 1900 than it had been in 1800. The construction of a spectacular bridge across the Danube enabled it to extend from the Buda Hills, crammed with handsome palaces and churches, across to the flat, featureless plain of Pest, which soon became the industrial, commercial and working-class section of the city. A similar pattern was also followed in Cologne, Bordeaux and Warsaw.

Various factors allowed these cities to grow so rapidly. Railways, steamships, canning and, after the 1880s, refrigeration, all enabled them to draw their food supplies from the whole world rather than simply the surrounding countryside. As a result, the traditional dependence of a city on its immediate surroundings was replaced by a sharp

TRAVELLING IN STYLE **The world's first electrically powered suspension railway was opened in Germany in 1901. Working-class passengers share a Paris omnibus with top-hatted members of the bourgeoisie.**

FLEECING SAILORS IN LIVERPOOL

THE ANONYMOUS captain of a New York liner in the 1850s explained how Liverpool port regulations exposed his crews to the unscrupulous locals:

❢ In London there is no law forbidding the use of fire and lights on board ships in the docks. The consequence is, that the captains and crews of foreign ships live on board, with all the comforts about them to which they are accustomed . . . by this system, the captain has the complete control of his crew . . . On arriving at Liverpool we generally lose two-thirds of our crew before we have been three days in port. I find it utterly impossible to attempt to keep the men on board at night without either fire or light . . . To get to the boarding houses they are obliged to pass through the most profligate and disreputable parts of town . . . they are waylaid by gangs of prostitutes and other bad characters; and sailors are not very well able to resist such temptation . . . In many instances they have not only spent all their money in gin shops and brothels, or been robbed, but they have pawned the last article of clothing they possessed . . . Every captain knows that a sailor at sea without proper clothes is of very little use . . . Not unfrequently there is but one pea jacket and a pair of mittens among a watch of 15 or 20 men, which passes from one to the other as the wheel is relieved. . . . ❢

GREAT WELCOME The whole town turns out in 1850 to watch the local MP and railway magnate George Hudson open new docks at Sunderland in England.

GIANT FAREWELL Brunel's *Great Eastern* was the largest ship ever built when it was launched in 1858. It was also the last major vessel built on the Thames.

divide between city and country. The contrast was accentuated by differences in their fabric as cheap iron, steel, concrete and glass transformed the way city folk lived and worked. Central heating, elevators, glass-roofed shopping arcades, apartment buildings, office blocks, swing bridges and pedestrian tunnels were all proof to country people of the gulf that separated them from city dwellers.

CURBING CRIME

People came to the cities in search of work. Not all of them found it, however, or kept it. Coming from America, where labour was permanently in short supply and almost any able-bodied man could find work of some sort, the young theological student Henry McLellan was totally unprepared for the experience of landing at Liverpool in 1832: 'A grim crowd awaited us there – 40 or 50 drivers held up their whip handles to engage our attention. "Coach, your honour." "Coach, sir" were reiterated by as many voices . . . Such a set of characters were perhaps never collected in our country. A dozen thrust themselves forward, "Shall I carry your baggage, your honour?", "your umbrella?" . . . [To] regard the group of ragged, wretched, lame and miserable creatures that had collected round us, as if we had

CITY OF GOLD SHOWS A GLITTERING FUTURE

STATELY DOME The hall housing Melbourne's International Exhibition of 1879 rivalled European grandeur.

INDUSTRY created new cities, wherever its demand for materials could penetrate and the goods it produced could be sold. Australia, half the world away from the cradle of the industrial revolution, supplied Britain with wool, wheat, meat – and gold. The fortunes generated by this trade supported the creation of cities which, unlike those of Britain's industrial North, were models of elegance and progressive living.

Melbourne was first settled in 1835, and in 1851 its future was assured when gold was discovered at Ballarat, 60 miles (97 km) away. Over the next 15 years, the goldfields of Victoria produced one-third of the world's output. Initially the impact on Melbourne was to denude it of its population. The Lieutenant-Governor wrote in wonderment to the British Colonial Secretary: 'Cottages are deserted, houses to let, business is at a standstill, and even the suburbs are closed. In some suburbs not a man is left.' The manager of a general store wrote: 'Men seemed bereft of their senses . . . Magistrates and constables, parsons and priests, merchants and clerks . . . all hastened to the diggings.' But soon he was placing orders with London for fine wines and fancy clothes. British exports to Australia rose 500 per cent in two years and Australia's population trebled in a decade.

A decade after the discovery of gold Melbourne had a population of 140 000, gaslighting, broad streets, gracious parks, botanical gardens, a university, an opera house that could seat 4000 and, in the race for the coveted Melbourne Cup, a national sporting institution. In 1877, Melbourne hosted the first cricket Test match between an English and an Australian side.

In 1879, the city spent £250 000 to stage an International Exhibition with 30 000 exhibits. At the city's cricket ground a game of soccer was played by electric floodlight as part of the celebrations. More to the point than these extravagant shenanigans, as a visiting Englishman observed, 'there is perhaps no town in the world where the ordinary working man can do better for himself and his family than he can in Melbourne'.

been the last resource upon which their hopes rested, this was enough to rend one's heart. . . . '

Those who could not find work begged, scavenged, stole or solicited. Crime was clearly linked with hardship. Discharged servicemen, toughened by their experience in the armed forces, undoubtedly accounted for the near-doubling indictable offences in England and Wales between 1816 and 1819 after the end of the Napoleonic Wars, and the unemployment and malnutrition that marked the

'Hungry Forties' saw a similar upsurge. In America, the influence of the Civil War was evident: in 1860 the prison population stood at 19 000; by 1870 at 33 000. Vagrancy legislation gave police considerable discretion in picking on those hapless souls who looked as though they might be potential offenders, and empowered them to prosecute such relatively harmless activities as playing ball games in a public place or making a slide on ice.

Throughout the 19th century, debate raged over whether criminals were the product of nature or nurture. A paper read at the annual meeting of the British Association for the Advancement of Science

THE NIGHT WATCH Before London's Metropolitan Police force was set up in 1829, the security of the capital's streets was in the hands of night watchmen, many of whom were elderly or infirm.

in 1869 sought to show that the skulls of habitual criminals were smaller than the average. Some scientists believed that there was not only a criminal 'personality' but even a criminal 'face', in which moral depravity was betrayed by the cast of the eyes or the set of the mouth.

Whether or not there was a discernible criminal type, few observers had any doubt that there was definitely a criminal class. Cities concentrated the

LAST REFUGE Families camp out in a New York police station around 1890. They are too poor to pay even the three cents a head that would have earned them the right to a bed in the hallway of a lodging house.

HOMELY DETAILS   Washing hangs outside and chickens rummage in the street in a London slum of 1889.

threat it posed, drawing together in their thousands both those who could not work and those who would not. One major solution was to set up and give more powers to police forces. The other was to work on the criminals themselves, and for this task a traditional institution was developed until it achieved an entirely new scale and form: the prison.

Until the industrial era, prison was used to incarcerate drunks until they sobered up, debtors until they paid up and accused persons until they were sent up before the judge. In general, only political offenders were given extended terms. Most other malefactors were punished by fines, flogging, humiliation or execution. Despite its constitutional provision against 'cruel and unusual punishments', even the USA was slow to phase these out. A forger in Massachusetts was pilloried and had his ears cropped at Salem in 1801; the state of Georgia ducked a 'common scold' in 1817. Colonial powers

had the added option of transporting criminals to overseas possessions.

As police forces became more efficient at apprehending criminals and alleged criminals, however, conviction and sentencing became more problematic. In Regency England, where over 200 offences carried the death sentence, juries became increasingly reluctant to return guilty verdicts. In the 1750s two-thirds of Londoners sentenced to death were actually executed, but half a century later the proportion had fallen to less than one in three.

As a result, more and more people were sent to prison. Isolated and regimented, the prisoner could be urged to repentance and compelled to conform to the work ethic by picking oakum or walking the treadmill. Prisons were a solution to a problem that most people thought of as essentially urban. Urban crime was more visible than rural crime and often more systematically organised. Fagin's juvenile

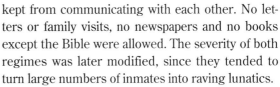

REPENTANCE AND RESETTLEMENT Right:
Condemned felons sing hymns around
a coffin in London's Newgate prison
before being hanged publicly outside.
Below: Female paupers are confined to
London's Bridewell reformatory.

gang in Dickens's *Oliver Twist* was no fantasy. In the England of the 1840s, nearly half of all detected crime was committed by the fifth of the population aged 15 to 24. Parkhurst Reformatory, established on the Isle of Wight in 1838, took as its first intake 102 boys under 18, most of them from London.

In the first half of the 19th century, the United States led the way in prison development. There was the 'Pennsylvania system', a regime that combined solitary confinement with hard labour. There was also the 'New York system' that allowed prisoners to come together to work but required them to maintain total silence at all times. Cells at the model Auburn Penitentiary were 7 ft (just over 2 m) deep, 7 ft high and half as wide, ventilated from above and without outside windows. Variations on these methods included wearing masks so that prisoners were unable to recognise one another, and chapels with strictly segregated seating so that prisoners could be preached at but still

kept from communicating with each other. No letters or family visits, no newspapers and no books except the Bible were allowed. The severity of both regimes was later modified, since they tended to turn large numbers of inmates into raving lunatics.

By the 1860s, however, Americans came to believe that their prison systems had fallen behind those of Europe. In many states corrupt politicians controlled all prison appointments; chain gangs in the South were notoriously abused. Under the influence of British models, the emphasis swung away from repentance and retribution towards reformation. In Britain, meanwhile, the rate of recorded crime fell from the 1860s until 1914, despite whole new categories of offences that were constantly being created: failure to send a child to school (1876), living off immoral earnings (1884), theatrical performances by children (1888), off-course betting (1906), the sale of alcohol to minors (1908). On the eve of the Great War, a quarter of London males aged 16 to 21 who were in prison were serving comparatively mild seven-day terms for such offences as drunkenness, gaming, obscene language, sleeping rough or riding a bicycle without lights.

PRICE OF PERJURY Confinement in
the pillory was last imposed in
England in 1830. Delaware in the
United States retained it until 1905.

TAMAR TRIUMPH

THE MASSIVE piers of the unfinished Tamar bridge dwarf the village of Saltash in the west of England. On the right, the final span rests on floats as it is manoeuvred into place. Isambard Kingdom Brunel's bridge, which would carry the Great Western Railway into Cornwall, required a central deepwater pier to support two spans, each 465 ft (142 m) long and weighing 1000 tons. The pier took 30 months to build, using a cast-iron cylinder, inside which workmen excavated the mud of the river bed. On September 1, 1857, Brunel, insisting on absolute silence and relying on signal flags to relay his instructions, orchestrated an army of men to raise the first span into position. It fitted to within 1/8 in (3 mm). In May 1859 Queen Victoria's husband, the Prince Consort, opened the bridge, naming it the Royal Albert Bridge. Brunel died the same year.

WOMEN IN THE CITY

For most women the coming of industry increased rather than diminished the triple burden of

adding to the household income while running a home and raising a family. At the same time,

growing numbers of women started to voice demands for fairer access to education and good jobs.

JOHN ADAMS, second president of the United States (from 1797 to 1801), usually paid careful attention to the opinions of his wife, Abigail. She advised him that 'in the new code of laws which I suppose it will be necessary for you to make, I desire you would remember the ladies, and be more generous to them than your ancestors. Do not put such unlimited power in the hands of husbands'. Nevertheless, on this matter he appears to have been singularly deaf.

As late as 1860 an American jurist pointed out that, although a wife's earnings belonged to her husband, she had no rights over his. If a wife was injured or slandered, compensation belonged to her husband, and if she died without making a will, her husband was entitled to all her personal property and a life interest in her real estate, whereas if he died intestate she was only entitled to a third of his. In Britain, women did not have the right to retain their own property after marriage until the passage of special Acts of Parliament in 1870 and 1882.

WIFE BEATING

Until 1850 almost every state in the United States recognised the legal right of a husband to beat his wife 'with a reasonable instrument'. One Massachusetts judge defined such an instrument as a 'stick no thicker than my thumb'.

In fact, Americans frequently stressed the elevated position of women in their society, but European observers were far from uniformly convinced. Alexis de Tocqueville noted that American girls did enjoy much freedom but thought that when they were married they were more circumscribed by their duties than their European counterparts. He also asserted that family relations in America had a greater intimacy and equality than in Europe. The Englishwoman Harriet Martineau noted acidly that the revered 'Founding Father' Thomas Jefferson had classified women with children and slaves as natural dependants of men.

In America, as in Britain, the first half of the 19th century witnessed many piecemeal initiatives to challenge and counter restrictions imposed on women's lives. Continental, especially Catholic,

STATUS SYMBOLS
In 1899, sociologist Thorstein Veblen argued that a man's wealth could be gauged by the number of women he supported in idleness.

EMPTY LIFE, FULL LIFE
Two paintings from the Edwardian period in Britain contrast the wretched loneliness of the exploited single women with the glowing contentment of a middle-class mother.

Europe lagged behind the English-speaking world in this respect. For many German moralists, a woman's life was circumscribed by '*Kinder, Kuche, Kirche*' (children, kitchen and church), and a popular preacher from Bremen, Friedrich Krummacher, boasted that 'My girls have never had what they call education. They know virtually nothing of our so-called literature, cannot speak a single foreign language . . .'. It was in reaction to attitudes such as these that the German women's movement focused almost entirely on pressing for the right to education. Even at the end of the 19th century, when American universities were modelling themselves on German ones, no German university admitted women as full students, and even women schoolteachers were forced to resign on marriage.

Preachers, teachers, politicians and editors on both sides of the Atlantic had long repeated the same message – the sanctity of the home, the purity

BUDGETING AT THE MARGIN

'MANAGING' remained a housewife's most crucial skill. The social investigator Charles Booth described how a London slum family of the 1890s stretched a meagre income:
❝ This family live to the greatest extent from hand to mouth. Not only do they buy almost everything on credit from one shop, . . . they every week put in and take out of pawn the same set of garments, on which the broker every time advances 16s, charging the, no doubt, reasonable sum of 4d for the accommodation. Fourpence a week, or 17s 4d a year, for the comfort of having a week's income in advance! On the other hand, even on credit they buy nothing until actually needed. They go to the shop as an ordinary housewife to her canisters: twice a day they buy tea, or three times if they make it so often; in 35 days they made 72 purchases of tea . . . Of sugar there are 77 purchases in the same time. ❞

BOURGEOIS BOHEMIANS In London, even artists like William Nicholson and his wife Mabel Pryde are portrayed in a setting of orderly comfort.

of womanhood, the fragility of femininity. But the tone was changed somewhat. In preindustrial times, the family had been trumpeted as a microcosm of society – simultaneously a miniature state, church and school, headed by a father who was king, priest and teacher. This was a world based on duty and authority.

During the course of the 18th century, however, people began to believe that family relations should be based on attraction and affection. English novelists, widely read on both sides of the Atlantic, ridiculed or demonised heavy-handed fathers and contrived their plots to ensure the triumph of 'true love'. As the British novelist Henry Fielding put it in *Tom Jones* : 'Love is the only foundation of happiness in the married state, as it can only produce that high and tender friendship which should always be the cement of the union.'

A survey of the extant American magazines published during the 30 years before the Revolution has revealed that at least a quarter contained a reference to romantic love; over the next 20 years the number of such references trebled. By the early 19th century, magazines were filled with articles making it plain that a man's best friend was his wife, rather than his dog, and that her duty was to be a limitless 'Source of Comfort and Spring of Joy'. *Sensible Etiquette* in its 16th edition (Philadelphia 1878) summarised the wifely function: 'To embellish the home and to make happy the lives of the near and dear ones who dwell within it.'

It must often have seemed a daunting task. The Rev T. DeWitt Talmage warned his female readers in the *Christian Herald* that every working day their husbands were engaged in nothing less than a battle: 'It is a wonder that your husband has any nerves or patience or suavity left . . . If he come home and sit down preoccupied, you ought to excuse him. If he do not feel like going out that night . . . remember he has been out all day . . . Remember, he is not overworking so much for himself as . . . for you and the children.'

Catharine Beecher, author of America's most popular book on household management, went even further when she assured her readers that they held in their hands nothing less than the fate of their democracy: 'The mother forms the character of the future man . . . the wife sways the heart, whose energies may turn for good or for evil the destinies of a nation.' The growth of industry brought new products and services that relieved better-off women of a range of wifely functions, while the actual equipment of housekeeping made her life easier, too. Light tinware replaced

TRENDSETTER The American Sarah Josepha Hale edited women's magazines, notably Godey's Lady's Book and Magazine (left), for almost 50 years.

AN AMERICAN NEWSPAPER SEES VIENNESE WOMEN AT WORK

AN AMERICAN journalist visiting the Austrian capital in 1873 expressed surprise at the sight of women doing 'men's work'. The parallel with the endless grind of life in the contemporary American West apparently escaped him:

❛ All the most menial work in Vienna is done by women, such as cleaning and sweeping the streets, gathering up garbage, carrying water, and pumping it from the cisterns to the reservoirs in the upper stories, sawing wood, spading the ground, the making and carrying mortar in buckets, and handling the brick used in building . . . [The women] are of all ages, young, middle-aged, and old; but all seem to be strong and healthy. ❜

triumphant visits to the United States, where she was received with acclaim by fellow feminists.

Partly as a result of such pioneering efforts, some professions began grudgingly to admit women to their ranks – education in particular. Quaker teacher and pioneer feminist Susan B. Anthony in America caused a furore when she pressed successfully for the right to contribute to an 1853 debate on the low status of the teaching profession. When the president of the convention, a West Point professor, reluctantly conceded her the platform, she tartly pointed out to him and the rest of the overwhelmingly male audience: 'Do you not see that so long as society says a woman is incompetent to be a lawyer, minister or doctor, but has ample ability to be a teacher, that every man of you who chooses that profession tacitly acknowledges that he has no more brains than a woman?'

Medicine proved an even more entrenched male bastion. The career of Elizabeth Blackwell, however, showed what could be achieved. Her Bristol family emigrated to New York when she was only 11 and at 17, when her father died, she and her sister helped to support the family by establishing a boarding school for girls. Meanwhile, through a combination of self-instruction and private tuition, she prepared herself for her chosen career. Rejected initially by medical schools in Pennsylvania and New York, she was finally accepted in

1847 at Geneva Medical College in New York. Two years later, Elizabeth Blackwell graduated at the head of her class as the first woman to gain the degree of MD from a medical school in the United States. Passing on to postgraduate study in Paris, she faced another bizarre requirement – that she don male attire to secure admission to classes and wards – which she resolutely declined to do. After further study at St Bartholomew's Hospital in London, she opened a practice in New York City.

Here in 1857, she established the New York Infirmary for Women and Children, a hospital staffed by women that subsequently became a pioneering centre of women's medical education. During the Civil War, Blackwell organised a unit of field nurses and in 1869 returned to her native country to help found the London School of Medicine for Women, where she became professor of gynaecology.

HOLD THE LINE, PLEASE! A German exchange in 1889. Running telephone exchanges rapidly became a virtually all-female occupation.

While exceptional women struggled for what were then regarded as exceptional rights, most women struggled to survive. Their contribution to the economy passed largely unrecorded. Most did two jobs – raising a family and contributing to its income when possible.

WORLDS OF WORK

Domestic service remained a major employer of female labour. In the 19th century, about a third of all European women were servants at some time in their lives, although no more than one in ten remained a servant throughout.

Some were relatively lucky. Service in a large aristocratic household, where servants – male as well as female – far outnumbered the family they worked for, could be comparatively easy-going; a few contemporary observers commented on the 'pampered' domestics of the super-rich. A more typical lot, however, was that recalled by one London maid: 'I went to Chiswick to work for a dentist and his wife. I was the only servant.

ALL IN THE NAME

The first American woman to keep her maiden name after marriage was the pioneer feminist Lucy Stone (1818-93). The eighth of nine children of a New York farmer, she financed herself through Oberlin College, lectured for the antislavery movement and helped to organise the first women's rights conventions in the 1850s. After her marriage 'Mrs Stone' and husband Henry B. Blackwell, brother of Dr Elizabeth Blackwell, helped to found the American Woman Suffrage Association and ran its weekly *Woman's Journal.*

I had to be up at 6 in the morning, and there were so many jobs lined up for me that I worked till 11 o'clock at night. I had to clean all the house, starting at the top and working down, sweeping and scrubbing right through. I was most conscientious. For breakfast I had bread and dripping. Dinner was herring, every day; tea was bread and marge. My room was in the attic. There was a little iron bed in the corner, a wooden chair and a washstand. It was a cold, bare, utterly cheerless room.'

The life of such a woman was hard, but at least she retained her 'respectability'. Other women were drawn into seamier occupations. Prostitution thrived in most industrial cities, while some women ended up in longer term but nonetheless extremely ill-defined relationships with men, as

OUTSIDE AND OUTSIDERS   A poor but respectable woman suns herself outside a secondhand furniture shop in London (left). Parisian 'courtesans' (above) flaunt their finery in the Bois de Boulogne.

REVOLUTION ON WHEELS Women cyclists in Paris. Active sports for women encouraged new, looser-fitting fashions.

their mistresses. Such relationships were normally loaded entirely in the man's favour – thanks to his greater power, wealth and status – among both the upper and middle classes and those lower down the social scale. A survey of some 8600 extramarital liaisons in the Paris of the 1830s and 40s shows that most of the men were artisans or shopkeepers, while nine-tenths of the women were servants or factory hands. Students from 'good' families routinely took seamstresses as their temporary companions while at college, abandoning them on graduation. In France, the frequency of transfers and the expense of supporting an absent wife induced many officers to postpone marriage until their retirement from active service. The army tolerated mistresses, provided a minimum of discretion was observed, and if the woman in question could entertain elegantly – in private. In rural areas, the

propertied single man often expected his 'housekeeper' to attend to his other needs, and female servants everywhere were often portrayed as hapless victims of their master's appetites, forced to choose between expulsion before or after dishonour.

Very occasionally local or family circumstances decreed that a wife, rather than a husband, should be a family's main breadwinner. One doughty London laundress filled in a mid-Victorian census return by putting herself first: 'head of family, mangling woman; John, husband, turns my mangle'. Retailing was another major sector in which women could do well. Describing his life in a Salford slum in northern England in the first decade of the 20th century, Robert Roberts made it clear that his family's corner shop, managed by his shrewd and determined mother, was their real source of support. Nominally it was owned by his father, a

VOTES FOR WOMEN! English suffragette Sylvia Pankhurst argues the case for women's votes in London in 1912.

skilled engineer but also a quarrelsome drunkard, who was frequently unemployed; in practice Mrs Roberts' keen ear and retentive memory for gossip enabled her to act as credit controller to her penurious clientele. Knowing whose man was in work, whose child was sick, who had pawned even their frying pan, she could judge quite accurately those who were likely to be able to pay off their 'slate' eventually.

Some women played an active, if rarely acknowledged, role in building up family businesses. The

great potter Josiah Wedgwood always looked to 'the approbation of my Sal' before committing a new design to production. And Jesse Boot, founder of the giant British pharmaceutical chain that still bears his name, was the grandson of a village 'wise woman'; his mother and sister gathered herbs in the countryside around Nottingham and helped make up the pills he sold over the shop counter.

CLUBBING TOGETHER

During the late 19th century not only did women assert their right to join movements, clubs and associations started by men but they also began to establish such institutions of their own. When the American socialite Julia Ward Howe was excluded

MINE EYES HAVE SEEN . . . Julia Ward Howe in 1902. She composed 'The Battle Hymn of the Republic' and was the first woman elected to the American Academy of Arts and Letters.

CLUTCHING AT STRAWS – A GOOD LUCK STORY

THE ENGLISH orphan Lucy Luck was brought up in a workhouse and endured several wretched jobs until she found work as a skilled straw-plaiter and married ploughboy Will. In 1869, Will, with three children to feed, asked his master for an increase on his weekly wage of 11s – for which he was given a month's notice to leave his cottage. Quitting Bedfordshire for London, he got work as a stable lad. Lucy and the children joined him later:

❝ I shall never forget my first two or three months in London. I think I cried most of the time, for my husband was on night work, and I amongst strangers . . . I would have given anything to have gone back to the country. I still kept on with the straw work, as the person I worked for sent it up from Luton once a week . . . [Later] I . . . worked at the shops in Westbourne Grove for 13 years. I was in the workroom part of the time and had my work at home the other part . . . After that I went to another place in the West End, where I worked for one gentleman for 20 years . . . I have been at the work for 47 years, and have never missed one season, although I have a large family . . . In my busy seasons I have worked almost night and day . . . The straw work is very bad, as a rule, from July up to about Christmas. During that time I have been out charring or washing, and I have looked after a gentleman's house . . . [and] taken in needlework. This was before any of my children were old enough to work. I have done my best to bring them up respectable . . . I have had my troubles with them, as any mother would have with a large family, but not one of them have brought us any sorrow or disgrace. ❞

from meeting Charles Dickens, she founded the New England Women's Club, in 1868, to establish a cultural forum under female control. After the American Civil War necessity forced thousands of educated women onto the labour market and into business in the shattered South. In the western states, women gained power from their scarcity value. In the 1860s there were four men for every woman in Washington state, eight in Nevada and 20 in Colorado – where any woman's job paid four times better than it would have done in Chicago, with room and board thrown in.

In 1869, the very year in which the American Woman Suffrage Association was formed back in the East, Wyoming granted the vote to women. In the Midwest, no longer a frontier but a region of settled farming, a new mass organisation emerged. Founded in 1867 as the Patrons of Husbandry but known colloquially as 'the Grange', it was part pressure group and part social club. By 1874, it had 1.5 million members. Women were admitted as equal members from the start and did much to ensure that its 15 000 branches spent as much time on 'socials', concerts and on building up libraries as on sending petitions to Congress in favour of lower freight rates. The Midwestern universities may have led the way in opening up higher education for women, but it was in the East that the first elite all-women's colleges were founded: Vassar, Smith

PIN MONEY NEEDLES A NATION'S CONSCIENCE
In 1906, the English Daily News sponsored a Sweated Industries Exhibition to expose exploitation. Matchbox makers like these might earn as little as 2d a day.

and Wellesley. It was in the East, too, that the associations became most diversified. By 1880 a correspondent to *Atlantic Monthly* could complain that there was almost too much choice: 'We have art clubs, book clubs, dramatic clubs, pottery clubs. We have sewing circles, philanthropic associations, scientific, literary, religious, athletic, musical and decorative art societies . . .'

ENTERTAINING THE PEOPLE

Ancient talents and new technologies combined to develop entertainment as an

industry catering for the needs of city-dwellers. As a result, people were

less and less participants in their own culture and more and more consumers of it.

THE AMUSEMENTS of the British seldom failed to amaze sophisticated continentals, such as the Frenchman Henri Misson, who recorded his impressions in 1719. Like dozens of other visitors, he was bemused both by the brutality of English pastimes and their popularity with the highest, just as much as the lowest, classes: 'Besides the Sports and Diversions common to most other European Nations, as Tennis, Billiards, Chess, Tick-Tack (backgammon), Dancing, Plays, etc, the English have some which are particular to them . . . Cock-Fighting is a Royal Pleasure . . . Combats between Bulls and Dogs, Bears and Dogs and sometimes Bulls and Bears . . . Anything that looks like

SYMPHONY OF THE STREETS Strolling musicians 'worked' different sections of a city each day. Winter meant hard times for most of them.

fighting is delicious to an Englishman. If two little Boys quarrel in the Street, then Passers-by stop, make a Ring round them in a Moment, and set them against one another, that they may come to Fisticuffs. . . .'

A reaction began to set in among the English themselves around the end of the 18th century when high-minded reformers began to call for 'rational recreation' and clergymen such as the Rev A. Macaulay spoke out against the debasement of traditional 'wakes' – local festivities in honour of the patron saint of a parish – in the North of England: 'The spirit of old English hospitality is conspicuous among the farmers on these occasions; but with the lower sort of people, especially in the manufacturing villages,

FUN IN THE SUN A sword swallower entertains the crowd on Hampstead Heath in 1898. The heath was a favourite bank-holiday gathering place for Londoners.

MOBILE MIRACLES This 'unique' American carousel was actually made in Britain. Performers of all kinds were highly mobile. Around 1900, more than 150 American singers, comedians and novelty acts – such as this band of singing midgets – were appearing on stage in London.

the return of the wake never fails to produce a week, at least, of idleness, intoxication and riot; these, and other abuses, by which these festivals are so grossly perverted from the original end of their institution, render it highly desirable to all the friends of order, of decency and of religion, that they were totally suppressed.' Suppression came only slowly, with laws passed in the 1830s.

In the countryside, the village inn remained the focus for cricket, skittles and other team games that lent themselves to intervillage contests. Chapel and church provided a venue for more decorous recreations such as choral singing, summer picnics, tea parties and 'improving' lectures by temperance campaigners or missionaries home on leave. In the United States, where churchgoing was more popular than in Britain, this was even more the case.

Markets and fairs also brought colour to the countryside, providing ready-made audiences for itinerant acrobats, jugglers, illusionists and musicians. In the 19th century, these elements were organised into the travelling circus, often accompanied by a menagerie of wild beasts. America had over 30 on the road by the 1830s.

In Britain, the time-honoured 'country sports' of hunting, shooting and fishing were reserved for the gentry and wealthier farmers. Labourers might enjoy the brilliant spectacle of a fox hunt or be employed as beaters on a shoot, but their own opportunities were limited by severe 'game laws', not to mention the hazards of man traps and spring

BRUTALITY AND THE BEAST Many beasts – like this bear performing in a London suburb in 1895 – were routinely beaten and starved into submissiveness.

guns. In the wildernesses of continental Europe, on the other hand, particularly the uplands of France, Spain and Italy, rough shooting flourished as a way of supplementing the pot with small game or birds.

In America, where hunting was a part of everyday life outside the big cities, marksmanship was a badge of manhood. Frontier amusements included the trotting race, knife-throwing and log-rolling. Wrestling was much favoured and almost devoid of rules; many contestants

cultivated long thumbnails as an aid to more effective eye-gouging. Women usually contented themselves with turning domestic tasks into social occasions by organising quilting bees, corn huskings and the like. Given the isolation, drabness and drudgery of most of their lives, any opportunity to gather and gossip was a welcome one.

URBAN BUT SELDOM URBANE
In the new industrial towns, leisure activities became more organised and commercialised. Most took place outside the home, which was invariably too small, too crowded or too dark to allow much scope for recreation beyond reading, card-playing or drinking. The better-off artisan might subscribe to a circulating

SAME SHOW, DIFFERENT SEATS
The poor (left) are herded together in 'the gods' of a Parisian theatre. The well-off (below) foregather outside the foyer before occupying the comfort of the circle or stalls.

P.T. BARNUM: SHOWMAN OF THE CENTURY

AT THE AGE OF 25 Phineas Taylor Barnum (1810-91) discovered his vocation when he exhibited a wizened black woman, Joice Heth, as the allegedly 161-year-old childhood nurse of George Washington. When a post-mortem examination subsequently proved her to be no more than 80, Barnum simply claimed he never knew.

In 1842, he acquired John Scudder's five-storey American Museum on Broadway, cleared out its conventional collection of stuffed animals and waxworks and filled the place with freaks and curiosities. The 'Feejee Mermaid' was a fake, but the Siamese twins, Chang and Eng, were genuine, as was the 25 in (64 cm) Charles S. Stratton, whom Barnum promoted as 'General Tom Thumb' and presented in person to such dignitaries as President Lincoln and Queen Victoria.

Barnum regarded himself as a man with a mission: 'This is a trading world and men, women and children, who cannot live on gravity alone, need something to satisfy their gayer, lighter moods and hours, and he who ministers to this want is in a business established by the Author of our nature.' The American Museum finally went out of business in 1868, after fires had all but destroyed it twice. In the

LARGER THAN LIFE   P.T. Barnum with 'Commodore' Nutt, from his American Museum.

quarter century of its existence it attracted 82 million visitors, including Charles Dickens and the future Edward VII.

In partnership with the modest but efficient James A. Bailey, Barnum went on to revolutionise the

HIS NAME LIVES ON The National Biscuit Company's animal-shaped crackers were launched in 1902 – more than a decade after Barnum's death.

traditional circus by vastly increasing its size to become 'the greatest show on earth'. Abandoning wagon transport in favour of the railway, he by-passed any town incapable of generating $5000 of business and in his first season took over $1 million. Emphasising the wholesomeness of this entertainment, he shrewdly distributed free passes to clergymen as well as newspaper editors.

Barnum lived in style in an Oriental mansion, 'Iranistan', in Bridgeport, Connecticut. He served two terms in the Connecticut state legislature and, as Mayor of Bridgeport, fought against prostitution and union labour discrimination against black workers. During his last illness, he had the bizarre satisfaction of reading his own obituary, printed in advance at his request by a New York newspaper.

library or attend 'improving' lectures, especially those enlivened by a 'magic lantern' show. He might also buy a musical instrument and join one of the brass bands that flourished throughout the North of England, in particular, from the 1840s onwards. Progressive employers were often willing to subsidise 'banding', recognising that it kept their workers from more violent and antisocial pursuits.

'Serious' theatre was the domain of the middle classes, and even among them its appeal was limited by its association with vice: actress was virtually a synonym for mistress, or worse, in the eyes of the ultra-respectable. The discriminating therefore often preferred to patronise concerts or the opera.

America's first purpose-built theatre was established in 1766, outside the city limits, and the jurisdiction, of Philadelphia; New York acquired one the following year. Both were condemned by some

TIME FOR A PINT The gaiety of a German beer garden in 1886 contrasts with the dinginess of an English pub.

contemporary moralists as 'synagogues of Satan'. Boston did not lift its ban on theatres until 1794. The city fathers' disapproval may have been well-founded: no sooner had theatres been permitted than the musicians employed in them placed a notice in the local press beseeching patrons not to bombard them with apples, stones and other missiles. In the first half of the 19th century, visits from great English acting dynasties such as the Kembles began to raise the theatrical tone and productions of Shakespeare became increasingly popular. By the mid-century there were over 40 American stage companies in existence, and American performers such as Charlotte Cushman and Edwin Forrest had begun to achieve the greatest dramatic accolade – triumph in London itself.

Lower-class townspeople on both sides of the Atlantic patronised what in England were called 'penny gaffs', where, on a makeshift stage, singers, dancers, tumblers and comedians battled to hold the attention of a boisterous and usually drunken audience. Over the century these crude entertainments developed into more polished and lavish, but still raucous, forms: music hall in Britain, burlesque and vaudeville in the United States, and cabaret in France. By 1868, London alone had 39

music halls, Birmingham nine, and Leeds and Manchester eight each. There were more than 220 over the rest of the country.

The town-dweller relaxed in a drinking establishment: the pub in Britain, the brasserie in France, the saloon in America and the beer garden in Germany. Whatever its name or local peculiarities, the tavern offered light, warmth, cheery banter and often games of chance and live music as well. By the second half of the 19th century, many pubs and saloons in large cities were handsomely built on commanding corner sites and appointed with brass and mahogany fittings, and etched-glass windows.

The quantities of liquor consumed were prodigious. In the 1790s, the average American over the age of 15 outdrank his English counterpart with an annual consumption of 34 gallons (155 litres) of beer or cider, 5 gallons (23 litres) of spirits and almost a gallon (4.5 litres) of wine. France's rising prosperity was matched by the increased consumption of brandy and, more damagingly, by absinthe, until its sale was banned by law in 1916 – the wormwood used to flavour it was believed to cause hallucinations and even sterility, though the cause of these symptoms may have been the high alcohol content: around 70 per cent in some cases. In Normandy the

An English Journalist Deplores German Waste

Henry Mayhew's *German Life and Manners as seen in Saxony* enjoyed great success in England in the 1860s. Here, he chronicles the 'unnecessary enjoyments' of Sundays and holidays:

❦ . . . it is the general custom in Eisenach for the citizens to begin dropping into the beer houses at 10 in the morning. Indeed, hardly a grown man in the town ever dreams of going to church – the congregation consisting almost entirely of the old women and children. After the midday dinner, a walk is usually taken to the suburbs, and a halt made at one of the beer gardens in the neighbourhood, or else a visit paid to the concert at the 'Fantasie' (a tavern in the outskirts so called), where, of course, more beer is drunk . . . After this the gentleman returns home to his supper . . . and immediately this is swallowed he retires to pass the remainder of the evening drinking, smoking, playing cards or billiards . . . at any one of the 40 different taverns in the town.

Next in the list come the holidays, of which there are 13 entire days in the course of the 12 months; and such is the general cessation from labour, that not even bread is baked at such times. Of these holidays, three occur at Christmas, one day at the New Year, three at Easter, three at Whitsuntide, one on Ascension Day and two on certain ordained days of so-called penance and fasting – the penance and fasting consisting, like the enjoyments on other holidays, in universal beer-drinking, smoking and gambling . . . the worship of Cambrinus (the German god of beer, whose portrait hangs in almost every tavern) is the chief idolatry of the country.

While dealing with the tavern habits of the Saxon people, it is important that we should not omit to mention the sums of money they are in the habit of spending either in cards, billiards or skittle-playing. Most of the citizens of Eisenach belong to some skittle club . . . and among the 40 beer houses in the town there are no less than 12 skittle-grounds . . . [and] at least eight billiard tables. . . .

But even as the beer-house habits of the Germans naturally beget habits of card-playing, billiard and skittle-playing . . . so does the love of gambling thus engendered give rise . . . to an utter distrust in those forms of industry and enterprise as the means of obtaining wealth, which are the marked characteristics of our countrymen. In Germany, however, the people . . . have lost all belief in self-reliance, and put . . . faith in lotteries as the means of amassing riches. . . . ❧

---

regular drink was coffee spiked with Calvados, the average household consuming 11 to 15½ gallons (50 to 70 litres) of spirits per year. The painters Degas and Toulouse-Lautrec both depicted chronic alcoholism as they knew it at first-hand, highlighting two novel and essentially urban incarnations of vice – the solitary drinker and the female drunk. In Britain, consumption per head peaked in the 1870s, declining slowly thereafter, though for millions it remained, in the proverbial phrase, 'the shortest road out of Manchester' and in 1900 there was still one public house for every 300 of the population.

A World on Wheels

Railway travel enabled the townsman to escape the town. The devout Baptist missionary Thomas Cook laid the foundations of a whole new service industry, package tourism, in the 1840s when he chartered a railway train to convey 500 people from Leicester to Loughborough in the English Midlands to hear a celebrated

Drink and Dine In a French cabaret of the 1850s wine is the standard drink, while hot, nourishing soup is also available.

FACTORY INSPECTORS PRAISE A SCOTTISH COMPANY

BY THE 1870s, British factory inspectors, initially appointed to enforce laws for safety at work and restricting working hours, were also commenting on workers' welfare:

❝ In visiting factories it is always pleasant to notice any efforts made by the occupiers to promote the social well-being and improvement of their work people. In this respect Messrs James Smieton & Sons, of the Panmure Works, Carnoustie, afford a praiseworthy example . . . In connection with these works is an elegant and spacious hall, capable of accommodating 600 persons, and furnished with piano and harmonium . . . There is also a reading-room on the premises . . . Five daily and weekly newspapers are supplied . . . A bagatelle table and chess and draughtboards are also placed in this room. A library, containing about a thousand well-selected volumes, has also been established . . . The factory and dwellinghouses are situated . . . in the immediate neighbourhood of an excellent golf course, where, during their leisure hours, the male workers may enjoy one of the most exhilarating outdoor games in the country. ❞

temperance lecturer. The railway companies were quick to seize on the potential for excursions, especially to the seaside. Some resorts, such as Scarborough and Brighton, had long catered for visitors who came, on medical advice, to benefit from the allegedly restorative properties of sea-bathing. Others, such as sedate Bournemouth and brash Blackpool, benefited from their new railway connections to inland cities. In France, Deauville and Biarritz became centres of summer sophistication. In America, the wealthy had Newport, Rhode Island; by the 1860s, its 15 000 residents were joined annually by 3000 people rich enough to take cottages, twice that number who stayed in various hotels and boarding houses, and tens of thousands who came on one-day excursions. New Yorkers trekked to Coney Island, even if it did take two and a half hours to get there by horsecar, ferry and boat before the opening of the Bay Ridge streetcar line in the 1880s.

SAFE TRAVEL **Railway and steamship travel underpinned the expansion of the tourist industry, led by such pioneers as Thomas Cook.**

Railways also made remote areas accessible to the hunter, the hiker and the naturalist. In Britain, they opened up the Lake District, Dartmoor and the Scottish Highlands. In America, shooting parties of the wealthy, sometimes escorted by famous figures such as 'Buffalo Bill' Cody or the frontiersman Kit Carson, penetrated the Great Plains to participate in the slaughter of herds of bison. A more protective measure came in 1879 when the Yellowstone area was designated as America's first National Park. Meanwhile, formerly remote and barren areas such as Colorado and Florida were beginning to capitalise on the attractions of their climate and scenery: Colorado Springs was founded in 1871, and in Florida the population of Jacksonville was doubling every winter by 1874. From the 1870s onwards, the less affluent inhabitants of the American North-east invented a cheaper version of the summer vacation by camping in the woods.

Railways were also essential to the success of the sort of event pioneered by the Great Exhibition of 1851. Staged in London's Hyde Park, it attracted over 6 million visitors and yielded a substantial profit, which was used to buy up market gardens lying to the south of its spectacular Crystal Palace and to create the present South Kensington museum complex. Paris followed suit with major 'Expositions' in 1855, 1862 and 1867. Philadelphia hosted a massive

Centennial Exhibition to mark America's first century of independence; exhibitors from 56 foreign nations and colonies took part. And Chicago, the hub of the American railway network, was the site chosen for the World's Columbian Exposition of 1892 to mark the 400th anniversary of Columbus's landfall in the New World.

A PASSION FOR SPORT

During the 19th century, sport became codified and professionalised. Britain took the lead in this process, to such an extent that formerly local bodies – the Marylebone Cricket Club, for example, and the Wimbledon Croquet and Lawn Tennis Club – became world authorities for their sports, just as the Jockey Club became the model for its American and continental counterparts. Boxing became synonymous with the Marquess of Queensberry, who in 1867 lent his name to a new code that stipulated the use of padded gloves and introduced the count of ten to determine a knockout.

English enthusiasts not only drew up rules and standards for sports invented in England, such as cricket, soccer, rugby, squash, badminton, bowls and snooker, but also imported sports, like golf from Scotland and hockey from France. The urge to codify was largely a result of new competitions that drew in sides, particularly school or college teams, from such wide areas that differing local usages soon became a potent cause of conflict.

Professionalisation developed as half-day working on Saturdays in Britain and America made it possible to organise matches that drew large paying crowds. In 1869, the Cincinnati Red Stockings became the first professional baseball team and revealed the superiority of the trained, full-time player by beating every team they met. The captain and manager of this enterprise was an Englishman, Harry Wright, who had been a professional player for the St George Cricket Club on Staten Island and coach to the Knickerbocker Baseball Club.

In Britain, soccer led the way. By the 1860s, competitions were being organised on a national basis, using the rules followed by the undergraduates of Cambridge University. In 1888, 12 professional English clubs formed a national league. London and the industrial cities of the North of England and Lowland Scotland established a dominance over

FIST FIRST John L. Sullivan won the world heavyweight championship in 1882 in a bareknuckle contest. A decade later, he lost it to 'Gentleman Jim' Corbett, fighting under Queensberry rules with gloves on.

ANGLO-AMERICAN AMUSEMENTS Professional baseball (above) was pioneered by an English cricketer. Croquet (right) was an English passion that was eagerly received on the East Coast.

147

SINGALONG AND SILENCE
Entertainers such as the stars of vaudeville and music hall commanded rapt attention – as depicted by the English painter Walter Sickert. Their songs (above) included both sentiment and satire.

the professional game they have never lost. By 1897, the leading competition match was the Football Association's Cup Final, attracting crowds of 65000.

Rugby, which originated as a form of football played at the English boarding school of that name, split from soccer in 1863, when the newly formed Football Association banned handling the ball, except by the goalkeeper. In the 1870s, it was promoted in the USA by Harvard men who had encountered it in Canada, but it soon developed into something very different and extremely hazardous as coaches selected players on the basis of their prowess as boxers and wrestlers. From these beginnings, American football was born. The first recorded professional game was played on August 31, 1895, at Latrobe in Pennsylvannia, when a team from Latrobe played one from the neighbouring town-

ship of Jeannette. The Latrobe players convincingly beat their rivals by 12 goals to 1.

Cycling was one of the few new pastimes to attract solid working-class participation in Britain. The invention of pneumatic tyres led in the 1880s to the 'safety bicycle', whose basic design has scarcely changed since then. Working men bought them because they roughly trebled the distance they could easily travel to work therefore vastly increasing the area in which they could seek employment. Having bought bicycles, usually by instalments, they also found them perfect for day-trips to the countryside at weekends. By the 1890s there were over 2000 cycling clubs and 1.5 million cyclists in Britain. The first cycle race, held in Paris in 1868, was won by an Englishman. Racing in America began a decade later, and the first Tour de France was held in 1903.

FADS ACROSS FRONTIERS

Recreations and institutions now taken for granted were once startling innovations. For example, the modern restaurant – a place where dining was as much a matter of entertainment as refreshment, and where the customer could select dishes from a menu – was essentially a by-product of the French Revolution. Restaurants were set up by the unemployed chefs of exiled or executed aristocrats.

The finest of these pioneering eating establishments was Antoine Beauvilliers's Grande Taverne de Londres in Paris. According to the gastronomic writer Jean-Athelme Brillat-Savarin, Beauvilliers would 'indicate here a dish to be avoided, there one

to be ordered immediately . . . and send, at the same time, for wine from the cellar . . . ; in short, he assumed so gracious and pleasing a tone, that all these extra articles seemed like as many favours granted by him'. For the next century, continental Europe conducted a culinary crusade across the English-speaking world. In 1831, for example, the Swiss Delmonico brothers opened New York's first eating place to operate on the menu system.

For most of the 19th century, fashions in pastimes usually went one way across the Atlantic, from Europe to America. A Swiss professor of law began to offer gymnastics instruction at Harvard in the 1820s. There were cricket matches between teams from New York, Philadelphia, Toronto and Montreal, until baseball, widely played in army camps on both sides during the Civil War, asserted itself as the national game. Tennis was introduced from England via Bermuda to become the fad of the 1870s, along with bicycling. The next sporting craze to cross the Atlantic was golf, introduced by Scots immigrants. Stage stars Sarah Bernhardt and Lily Langtry made high-profile tours of the USA in the 1880s and Gilbert and Sullivan's 'Savoy Operas' swept through the land in the same decade.

But by then the tide was turning. In 1887, Buffalo Bill's 'Wild West Show' took London by storm, making the owner 'a barrel of money' – $ 1.4 million in one summer. A directory of Americans resident in London in 1901 listed more than 160 vaudeville performers, from sharpshooters to trick cyclists to 'musical blacksmiths' – not to mention one Harry Houdini, the 'Handcuff King'.

RED WINDMILL The exotic exterior of the Moulin Rouge (left) suggests a world of glamour and wonders. The posters of Henri de Toulouse-Lautrec (above) linger on the attractions within.

TIME CHART

WORLD EVENTS

SHOWCASE CITY   Peter the Great's new capital, St Petersburg.

1700-21 The Great Northern War accelerates the decline of Sweden and the rise of Russia as a great power.

1701-14 The War of the Spanish Succession. Britain takes Gibraltar in 1704 and the Duke of Marlborough defeats the French at Blenheim.

1707 England and Scotland are united by the Act of Union. Scotland retains its own legal, educational and religious institutions.

1712 Peter the Great transfers the Russian capital from Moscow to St Petersburg.

1714 George I becomes the first Hanoverian ruler of England – he will reign until 1727.

1720 The British South Sea Trading Company collapses (the 'South Sea Bubble'), ruining thousands of speculators.

1732 Georgia, the last of the 13 American Colonies, is founded as a penal colony for London criminals.

**BUBBLE MANIA
The events of the 'South Sea Bubble' lampooned on playing cards.**

1736 Chien Lung becomes Emperor of China. His long reign (until 1796) sees 'the Celestial Empire' at the height of its prosperity and self-confidence.

1755 An earthquake in Lisbon kills 60 000 people.

1756 Outbreak of the Seven Years' War (1756-63). Britain establishes its colonial supremacy, driving the French out of both Canada and India.

LEISURE AND LEARNING

1701 Yale College is founded as a stronghold of Puritan orthodoxy.

1702 The *Daily Courant*, the first English daily newspaper, is published.

1709 The piano is invented by a Florentine harpsichord maker, Bartolomeo Cristofari.

1734 The first horse race in America is organised at Charleston Neck, South Carolina.

1737 Karl Linnaeus develops his system of plant classification and establishes the science of botany.

1746 Princeton is founded.

1749 Sign language for deaf mutes invented in Portugal.

1751-72 In France, the *Encyclopédie*, edited by Denis Diderot and Jean

**ALL USEFUL KNOWLEDGE
D'Alembert (left) and Diderot (right), editors of the Encyclopédie.**

d'Alembert, seeks to summarise all useful knowledge.

1753 The British Museum is founded.

1755 Samuel Johnson's *Dictionary of the English Language* is the first to include etymology, pronunciation and usage alongside definitions.

1759 Kew Gardens near London are set up as a centre for botanical study.

THEATRE AND MUSIC John Gay's *The Beggar's Opera* (1728); J.S. Bach's *St Matthew Passion* (1729); G.F. Handel's *Water Music* (1717) and *Messiah* (1742).

BOOKS Daniel Defoe's *Robinson Crusoe* (1719); Swift's *Gulliver's Travels* (1726); Fielding's *Tom Jones* (1749); Voltaire's *Candide* (1759).

LIFESTYLES AND TECHNOLOGY

STREET WISE   England starts using numbers to identify buildings.

1706 Carriage springs are invented, by Englishman Henry Mill.

1708 The numbering of houses begins in England, though widespread illiteracy means that painted signs and the like are still used for businesses.

1709 In England, Abraham Darby uses coked coal – instead of charcoal – to smelt iron. This makes iron cheaper to produce, so that iron is used more extensively in tools, machines, bridges and buildings.

A regular monthly postal service is set up between Bristol and New York.

1710 The Meissen porcelain works are founded in Saxony under the patronage of Elector Frederick Augustus I.

1714 German physicist Gabriel Fahrenheit constructs the mercury thermometer.

1727 Coffee – until now cultivated almost exclusively in Yemen – is first planted in Brazil.

1730 In England, Viscount 'Turnip' Townshend popularises crop rotation.

1733 John Kay invents the flying shuttle. It increases the speed of weaving and the width of cloth woven.

1745 Robert Bakewell develops selective breeding of livestock.

1756 The Sèvres porcelain factory is established under French royal patronage.

1760 The Wedgwood pottery works at Etruria open.

**LUXURY GOODS
A Meissen figurine.**

1761 – 1800

MIGHTY EMPRESS Catherine the Great of Russia.

1762 Catherine the Great proclaims herself Empress of Russia.

1769-70 British explorer Captain James Cook discovers Australia's east coast.

1773 The 'Boston Tea Party' is followed by the American Declaration of Independence in 1776. The ensuing Revolutionary War lasts until 1783.

1777 The new United States adopts the 'Stars and Stripes' as its flag.

1783 William Pitt the Younger, aged 24, becomes British Prime Minister.

1788 The 'First Fleet' of convict ships arrives at Botany Bay, Australia.

1789 In France the collapse of royal finances leads to a political crisis. The storming of the Bastille prison and the newly formed Constituent Assembly's Declaration of the Rights of Man lead to outright revolution.

1793 In France, the execution of Louis XVI and Marie Antoinette is followed by a 'Reign of Terror'.

1798 Horatio Nelson destroys a French fleet at the Battle of the Nile.

1799 Napoleon Bonaparte proclaims

BLOW FOR FREEDOM French revolutionaries storm the fortress-prison of the Bastille.

himself First Consul of France.

1800 The US government relocates from New York to Washington.

1768 The Royal Academy of Arts is established in London with Sir Joshua Reynolds as its first president.

1768 The first edition of the *Encyclopaedia Britannica* is published in Edinburgh.

1776 *The Wealth of Nations* by Adam Smith argues the virtues of an economy in which state interference is reduced to a minimum.

1776 Wilton House, Salisbury, is the first British stately home to be opened to the public.

SCOT FREE Adam Smith argued the case for 'free-market' economics.

1780 Diomed wins the first Derby at Epsom near London.

1781 The English astronomer William Herschel discovers Uranus.

1788 The first edition of the London *Times* is published.

1792 In France, Rouget de Lisle composes 'La Marseillaise'.

1793 The world's first public zoo opens at Jardin des Plantes, Paris.

1794 In America, Eli Whitney invents the cotton gin, improving the speed with which raw cotton can be processed, and cutting the cost.

1796 The English doctor Edward Jenner pioneers vaccination as a much safer method of preventing smallpox.

1798 *Essay on the Principle of Population* by the Englishman T.R. Malthus predicts that human population crises are inevitable as numbers increase until cut back by famine and disease.

MUSIC AND THEATRE Mozart's *The Marriage of Figaro* (1785), *Don Giovanni* (1787) and *The Magic Flute* (1791); Haydn's *The Creation* (1798); Beethoven's Symphony No 1 (1799).

BOOKS Laurence Sterne's *Tristram Shandy* (1767); Goethe's *The Sorrows of Young Werther* (1774); Rousseau's *Confessions* (1781); Laclos' *Les Liaisons dangereuses* (1782); Boswell's *Life of Samuel Johnson* (1791); Wordsworth and Coleridge's *Lyrical Ballads* (1798).

STEAM FACTORY Boulton and Watt's works at Soho in Birmingham, England.

1761 The Bridgewater Canal in Lancashire opens; it is Britain's first wholly artificial canal.

1764 In Britain, James Watt invents

the separate condenser which doubles the fuel-efficiency of steam engines. He later invents a gearing system to convert reciprocating (up-and-down) action into rotary motion.

James Hargreaves invents the spinning jenny.

1771 Richard Arkwright opens the world's first water-powered factory at Cromford, Derbyshire.

1774 Joseph Priestley discovers oxygen.

1779 The world's first cast-iron bridge is built at Ironbridge, England.

Iron enthusiast John Wilkinson

LIFT OFF The Montgolfier brothers' hot-air balloon.

demonstrates that iron boats will float.

1783 The first manned flight takes place, in a balloon designed by the French Montgolfier brothers.

1785 Benjamin Franklin invents bifocal spectacles.

The first lifeboat is patented in London.

1793 The French National Assembly introduces the metric system.

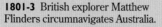

1801 – 1835

WORLD EVENTS

1801-3 British explorer Matthew Flinders circumnavigates Australia.

1803 The USA nearly doubles in size when it buys Louisiana from France.

1804 Napoleon crowns himself French Emperor.

1804-6 US army officers Meriwether Lewis and William Clark explore the American West.

1805 Nelson defeats a French-Spanish fleet off Cape Trafalgar.

1812-13 Napoleon invades Russia, but is forced to retreat after taking Moscow.

1812-15 War between the USA and Britain; British troops burn the new

MILITIA BLOODBATH The massacre of 'Peterloo' in Manchester.

American capital, Washington.

1815 Napoleon is defeated at Waterloo, in Belgium.

1819 In Britain, demonstrators

CHINA POLITICIAN
Sir Robert Peel set up London's Metropolitan Police force in 1829.

against government policies are sabred by yeomanry at the massacre of 'Peterloo'.

1830 In a year of revolutions the Duke of Orleans, Louis-Philippe, becomes French king.

1832 Reform of the British Parliament extends voting rights.

1833 Slavery is abolished in the British Empire.

1835 In Africa, the Boers start the Great Trek inland from the Cape.

LEISURE AND LEARNING

1801 The first Ordnance Survey maps are published in the UK.

1812 The Parthenon Marbles are brought from Athens to London by Lord Elgin.

1819 The first Highland Games are held in Scotland.

PEERLESS PLEASURE
Brighton Pier, on England's south coast.

1821 John Constable paints *The Hay Wain*. His example will later inspire French painters to begin painting directly from nature.

The mouth organ is invented in Berlin.

1823 The first pleasure pier is opened, at Brighton, England.

Rugby football originates at Rugby School, England.

1826 University College, London, is founded as England's first new university since the Middle Ages.

1831 Charles Darwin accompanies the *Beagle* on its voyage (1831-6) round the world. His observations lead him to formulate the theory of evolution through natural selection.

MUSIC AND THEATRE
Beethoven's Symphonies No 5 & 6 (1808); Rossini's *Barber of Sevill*e (1816); Schubert's *Trout Quintet* (1819); Mendelssohn's *Overture to 'A Midsummer Night's Dream'* (1826).

BOOKS Washington Irving's *Rip van Winkle* (1809); the Brothers Grimm's *Fairy Tales* (1812); Jane Austen's *Pride and Prejudice* (1813); Byron's *Don Juan* (1817-23); Mary Shelley's *Frankenstein* (1818); Sir Walter Scott's *Ivanhoe* (1820); Noah Webster's *American Dictionary of the English Language* (1828).

LIFESTYLES AND TECHNOLOGY

TRENDSETTER Trevithick's railway locomotive shows its paces.

1807 Fruit-flavoured carbonated soft-drinks are first manufactured, in Philadelphia.

1808 Richard Trevithick organises first public demonstration of a railway locomotive, in London.

WORKOUT
Babbage's 'difference engine'.

1811 London becomes the world's first city with a recorded population of more than a million.

1812 Cotton sewing thread is manufactured for the first time in Paisley, Scotland.

1816 The stethoscope is first devised in Paris to preserve the modesty of female patients.

1823 Charles Macintosh develops the first rainproof garments, and the next year the first inflatable life jacket for Sir John Franklin's Arctic expedition.

1823 Charles Babbage invents a calculating machine – ancestor of the computer.

1825 In England, the Stockton and Darlington Railway offers the world's first passenger service.

1829 Louis Braille devises a reading system for the blind.

1831 Michael Faraday devises a dynamo for generating electricity.

1834 In the USA, Cyrus Hall McCormick patents a mechanical reaper.

REAPING REWARDS Many early agricultural machines were developed in the United States.

1836 – 1865

UPRISING Revolution shakes Vienna in 1848.

1836 Texas wins independence from Mexico; it will join the USA in 1845.

1837 Victoria becomes Queen of Britain (until 1901).

1845-6 Potato blight leads to famine in Ireland, leaving a million people dead and leading to massive emigration, mostly to North America.

1847 Members of the Mormon Church found Salt Lake City in Utah.

1848-9 Revolutions across Europe. In France Louis Napoleon, nephew of Bonaparte, becomes president. He will proclaim himself Emperor Napoleon III in 1852.

1851 The gold rush boosts emigration to Australia.

1853 A US expedition led by Commodore Matthew Perry forces Japan to open its doors to foreign trade and diplomatic relations.

1854-6 Britain, France and Piedmont defeat Russia in Crimean War.

UNCLE SAM'S INVITATION The US Navy off Japan.

1857-8 British rule in India survives a major uprising – the Indian Mutiny.

1860-1 Italy is largely united under the Piedmontese royal family.

1861-5 Civil War in the United States. Abraham Lincoln proclaims the end of slavery in 1863 and is assassinated in 1865.

1864 The Geneva Convention sets up the Red Cross to mitigate the horrors of war. It is the brainchild of Swiss humanitarian Jean-Henri Dunant.

WORLD EVENTS

COOK'S TOUR The beginning of package tourism.

1837 In Britain, Isaac Pitman invents shorthand, and in the USA, Samuel Morse invents his code.

1839 Travellers discover remains of Maya culture in Central America.

1841 Thomas Cook organises the first ever railway excursion.

1843 The world's first nightclub, Le Bal des Anglais, opens in Paris. In New York, Mitchell's Olympic Theatre pioneers matinees.

1851-3 *The Stones of Venice* by John Ruskin defends Gothic art and medieval standards of craftsmanship, inspiring William Morris and others to challenge the value of mechanised production.

1859 Jules Leotard performs the first flying-trapeze circus act in Paris.

THEATRE AND MUSIC Verdi's *La Traviata* (1853); Donizetti's *Don Pasquale* (1843); Wagner's *The Flying Dutchman* (1843) and *Tristan and Isolde* (1865).

BOOKS Dickens' *Pickwick Papers* (1837); Stendhal's *The Charterhouse of Parma* (1839); E.A. Poe's *Murders in the Rue Morgue* (1841); Hawthorne's *The Scarlet Letter* (1850); Melville's *Moby Dick* (1851); Harriet Beecher Stowe's *Uncle Tom's Cabin* (1851-2);

SHOCK HORROR An illustration from *Uncle Tom's Cabin*.

Thomas Hughes' *Tom Brown's Schooldays* (1857); Kingsley's *The Water Babies* (1863); Lewis Carroll's *Alice's Adventures in Wonderland* (1865); Longfellow's *Song of Hiawatha* (1855); Tolstoy's *War and Peace* (1864-9).

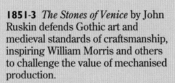

LEISURE AND LEARNING

EMPIRE SAUCE 'Worcester sauce' imitated a traditional Indian recipe.

1837 The first kindergarten is opened in Germany.

Worcestershire Sauce is first made by pharmacists Lea & Perrins of Worcester, England.

1840 A uniform penny post system is pioneered in Britain.

1843 Soap powder is first marketed, in New York.

1846 The first operation under anaesthetic is performed in the USA.

1851 The hypodermic syringe is invented in Lyons, France. The Singer sewing machine is manufactured, in Boston.

1853 German immigrant Levi Strauss popularises 'jean trowsers' among California goldminers.

1854 The paraffin lamp is invented in New York.

1856 The Bessemer process, devised by Englishman Henry Bessemer, makes steel cheaper to mass-produce.

1857-65 The USA and Britain are linked by Atlantic Cable.

1859 The first oil well is discovered in the United States.

KINDERGARTEN The Germans pioneered learning through play.

1862 The world's first underground railway – the Metropolitan Line from Paddington to Farringdon – opens in London.

1865 Rubber Wellington boots are first manufactured in Edinburgh.

LIFESTYLES AND TECHNOLOGY

1866 – 1890

WORLD EVENTS

LIFELINE The Suez Canal was the world's most strategic waterway.

1867 The USA buys Alaska from Russia for $7.2 million. Canada becomes a self-governing dominion within the British Empire.

1868 In Japan, the 'Meiji Restoration' overthrows the last dynasty of shoguns in the name of the emperor and inaugurates radical modernisation.

1869 The opening of the Suez Canal cuts six weeks off the voyage from Britain to India.

1870-1 The Franco-Prussian war leads to fall of the French Second Empire and the siege of Paris. Germany is united under Prussia.

REAL EMPEROR Bismarck manipulates Europe's crowned heads.

1876 General Custer's army is wiped out by native American forces at the Battle of the Little Bighorn.

1883 Eruption of Mount Krakatoa, Indonesia, killing some 36 000 people.

1887 Queen Victoria celebrates her Golden Jubilee.

LEISURE AND LEARNING

1866 The actor-manager Henry Irving makes his London stage debut.

1867 The first paperback book series is published in Leipzig.

1870 German archaeologist Heinrich Schliemann begins the excavation of Troy in Turkey.

1874 The first Impressionist exhibition is held in Paris.

1876 The first complete performance of Wagner's Der Ring des Nibelungen takes place at Bayreuth.

1877 English and Australian cricket teams play their first Test Match.

1880 The French sculptor Auguste

ANYONE FOR . . . ? Everybody wanted to be playing tennis.

RETURN MATCH The Australian touring team in England, 1878.

Rodin creates 'The Thinker'.

1884 The Oxford English Dictionary is published for the first time.

1887 A Study in Scarlet by Arthur Conan Doyle, the first Sherlock Holmes story, is published.

1888 Vincent van Gogh paints The Yellow Chair.

THEATRE AND MUSIC Ibsen's Peer Gynt (1867); Johann Strauss the younger's The Blue Danube (1867); Bizet's Carmen (1875); Brahms' Symphony No 1 (1876); Tchaikovsky's 1812 Overture (1882); Gilbert and Sullivan's The Mikado (1885).

BOOKS Jules Verne's Round the World in 80 Days (1874); Hardy's Far From the Madding Crowd (1874); Mark Twain's The Adventures of Tom Sawyer (1875); Dostoyevsky's The Brothers Karamazov (1880); R.L. Stevenson's Treasure Island (1883); H. Rider Haggard's King Solomon's Mines (1885); Zola's Germinal (1885); H.G. Wells' The War of the Worlds (1889).

LIFESTYLES AND TECHNOLOGY

1866 Alfred Nobel invents dynamite.

1867 In Britain, Joseph Lister pioneers antiseptic surgery.

1868 The gas hot-water geyser is invented in London.

1869 The first postcards are introduced, in Austria.

In the USA, the first coast-to-coast railway link is completed.

1874 The patenting of barbed wire revolutionises the management of livestock in America and Australia.

1876 Alexander Graham Bell invents the telephone. The next year, Thomas

FIXING TIME Time is regulated around the Greenwich Mean.

Edison invents the phonograph.

1878 In Britain, Joseph Swan invents a successful carbon-filament light bulb.

The first shipload of chilled meat is successfully exported from Argentina to Europe.

1879 The cash register is invented in Ohio.

1884 Evaporated milk is patented in St Louis, Missouri.

Greenwich Mean Time is adopted as the world standard and 'time zones' are devised.

1886 The Canadian Pacific Railway is completed.

Coca-Cola is launched as an 'Esteemed Brain Tonic and Intellectual Beverage' in Atlanta, Georgia.

1888 George Eastman perfects 'Kodak' box camera.

CASHING IN Machines invaded business and home life.

THE EDISON NEW STANDARD PHONOGRAPH PRICE $20 COMPLETE

1891 – 1914

WORLD EVENTS

1891 The Trans-Siberian Railway is started. It is completed in 1904.

1896 The first modern Olympic Games are held in Athens.

1897 The Klondike gold rush begins in northern Canada.

1898 Spanish-American war. Spain cedes Cuba, Puerto Rico, Guam and the Philippines to the USA for $20 million.

1899-1902 War erupts in South Africa between the Boers and British.

HEADLINE NEWS French reports on Russia's 1905 uprising.

Le Petit Journal

DISASTER Firestorms in San Francisco after the 1906 earthquake.

1900-1 The antiforeign 'Boxer Rising' in China is crushed by an international relief force.

1903 The Wright brothers make the first powered flight, lasting 12 seconds, at Kittyhawk, North Carolina.

1905 Unrest in Russia – the 1905 Revolution – is suppressed.

1906 An earthquake in San Francisco kills 700 people.

1909 Louis Bleriot flies across the English Channel.

1911 Norwegian Roald Amundsen's expedition beats Captain Scott's British party in the race to reach the South Pole.

1912 SS *Titanic* sinks on her maiden voyage; 1513 of its passengers are drowned.

1914 World War I breaks out in Europe.

UNSINKABLE Collecting for Titanic victims.

LEISURE AND LEARNING

1891 Toulouse-Lautrec designs his first posters for Montmartre music halls.

Basketball is developed at the YMCA, in Springfield, Massachusetts.

1893 The *Studio* magazine spreads the 'art nouveau' style in Britain.

The first Ferris wheel steals the show at the Chicago Exposition.

1894 Striptease is invented in Paris.

1895 Volleyball is developed at the YMCA in Holyoke, Massachusetts.

1897 London's Tate Gallery opens. The Carnegie Music Hall opens in New York.

1899 The golf tee is patented in Boston.

1903 The first Tour de France bicycle race is held.

1907 The first Cubist exhibition is held in Paris.

1910 Steel-shafted golf clubs are patented in New York.

1911 Irving Berlin's Alexander's Ragtime Band heralds a new era in popular music.

1913 The first Chelsea Flower Show is organised.

MUSIC AND THEATRE Dvorak's Symphony No 9 'From the New World' (1893); Wilde's *The Importance of Being Earnest* (1895); Chekhov's *The Seagull* (1896); Shaw's *Caesar and Cleopatra* (1898); Elgar's *Enigma Variations* (1899); Puccini's *Madame Butterfly* (1904); Lehar's *The Merry Widow* (1905).

BOOKS Kipling's *The Jungle Book* (1894); Anthony Hope's *The Prisoner of Zenda* (1894); Joseph Conrad's *Lord Jim* (1900); Beatrix Potter's *The Tale of Peter Rabbit* (1902); J.M. Barrie's *Peter Pan* (1904); Baroness Orczy's *The Scarlet Pimpernel* (1905); Kenneth Grahame's *The Wind in the Willows* (1908); Lucy M. Montgomery's *Anne of Green Gables* (1908); Edgar Rice Burroughs' *Tarzan of the Apes* (1914).

FERRIS WHEEL Chicago, 1893.

LIFESTYLES AND TECHNOLOGY

OLD AGE PENSIONS

OLD AGE British pensions began in 1909, a generation after Germany introduced them.

1891 Toothpaste is first marketed in a tube in Britain. The first electric torch is made in Bristol and the first electric kettle in St Paul, Minnesota.

1892 The first Primus stoves are manufactured in Stockholm.

1893 The first driving tests are introduced in Paris.

1895 King C. Gillette invents the safety razor.

Moving film is demonstrated in Paris by the brothers Auguste and Louis Lumière.

X-rays are discovered by the German Wilhelm Conrad Rontgen.

In Britain, Guglielmo Marconi invents radio telegraphy.

1896 The first purpose-built shopping centre is opened, in Baltimore.

1898 Cornflakes are first manufactured, as a health food, in Battle Creek, Michigan.

1903 James L. Kraft of Chicago manufactures processed cheese.

1903 The first sleeping pills are marketed by Bayer of Germany. Other examples of German inventiveness include the Thermos flask (1902), the household detergent Persil (1907) and the use of zips in clothing (1912).

1908 The first 'Model T' Ford is manufactured.

1911 The first Hollywood film studio is established.

SILENT SLAPSTICK The cinema created new forms of comedy.

INDEX

ACKNOWLEDGMENTS

ABBREVIATIONS
T=Top; M=Middle; B=Bottom;
R=Right; L=Left.

A.K.G.=Archiv für Kunst und Geschichte, London
B.A.L.=Bridgeman Art Library, London
E.T.A.=E.T.Archive, London
M.E.P.L.=Mary Evans Picture Library
R.H.P.L.=Robert Harding Picture Library.
S.M.=The Science Museum/Science & Society Picture Library.
T.B.A.=Toucan Books Archives.

1 S.M. 2-3 *The Iron-Rolling Mill*, painting by Adolph von Menzel, 1872-75, National Gallery, Berlin/A.K.G, London/ Photography Eric Lessing. 4 Arthur Lockwood, TL; M.E.P.L., TR; A.K.G., London, MR. 5 The Granger Collection, TL; E.T.A.,TR; Ullstein Bilderdienst, MR; S.M., BL; The Sutcliffe Gallery, Whitby, BR. 6 T.B.A. 7 *An Iron Forge*, 1893, painting by F. Cormon, Musée D'Orsay, Paris/Giraudon, TL; Harlingue-Viollet, TR. 8 E.T.A. 9 *Bishopton Rock Cutting, Glasgow*, Elton Collection/Ironbridge Gorge Museum, TL; William Mackenzie, engraving by G.R. Ward, 1845, Broad and Narrow Gauge Locomotives, T.R. Crampton, Collection of The Institution of Civil Engineers, from Mackenzie-Giant Of The Railways, exhibition catalogue written and compiled by M.M. Chimes, M.K. Murphy, G. Ribeil sponsored by Railtrack and its suppliers, BL, BR. 10 Kugelfischer G. Schäfer, Schweinfurt, TL; Arthur Lockwood, BL. 11 BASF, Ludwigshafen, TL; The Granger Collection, TR. 12 From the trade catalogue of Silber & Fleming, *c.* 1880s/ The Victorian Catalogue Of Household Goods, introduced by Dorothy Bosomworth, published by Studio Editions, 1991, TL, ML, BR; A.K.G., London, TR. 13 Arthur Lockwood. 14 *Suburban Railway Station*, *c.* 1890s, painting by G. d'Espagnat, Musée D'Orsay, Paris/Lauros-Giraudon/ ADAGP, TR; T.B.A., TL; Arthur Lockwood, BR. 15 Leicester Museums and Art Gallery, photograph by S.W.A. Newton, 1890s. 16 Porcelain figurine, made for the Imperial Porcelain Factory, St Petersburg, *c.* 1780, Musée D'Art et D'Histoire, St Germain-en-Laye/B.A.L., T; T.B.A., BL; E.T.A., BR . 17 T.B.A. 18-19 Illustration by Peter Morter. 19 T.B.A., BR. 20 *St Crispin's Day*, by George Cruikshank, from The Comic Almanack, 1836/T.B.A. 21 *Josiah Wedgwood I*, white on pale blue Jasper, after 18th century original by William Hackwood; *View of the Etruria Factory; A Thrower at Etruria Factory with Female Assistant*, *c.* 1900s/ The Trustees of the Wedgwood Museum, Barlaston, Staffordshire, England, TL, TR, ML; 21 Illustration by Kate Simunek, B. 22 M.E.P.L., T, M; 23 Arthur Lockwood, TL; E.T.A., BR. 24 Arthur Lockwood. 25 Courtesy of Jonathan Silver and Salts Estates Limited, TL, TR; Bradford Industrial Museum, MR; Bolling Hall Museum, Bradford, B. 26 Stadt Essen. 27 E.T.A., TL; Topham Picture Source, TR; Ironbridge Gorge Museum, MR, BL; *An Iron Forge*, 1772, painting by Joseph Wright of Derby, Broadlands Collection, Hampshire, BR. 28 M.E.P.L. 29 *Coalbrookdale at Night*, *c.*1800, painting by P.J. Loutherbourg/S.M., T; Arthur Lockwood, BL; Brunel University Library, MR. 30-31 Illustration by Paul Wright. 32 R.H.P.L./Photograph by Donald McLeish, TR; Barge Haulier, 1890, painting by Theodoor Verstraete, Musée des Beaux-Arts, Tournai, BL. 33 *Removal of the Broken Crucible*, 1884, painting by Constantin Meunier, Musées Royaux des Beaux-Arts de Belgique, Musée Constantin Meunier, Brussels. 34 Arthur Lockwood. 35 Arthur Lockwood, T; International Museum of Photography at George Eastman House, B. 36 *Distribution of the Bread in the Village*, 1892, painting by Frans van Leemputten, Koninklijk Museum voor Schone Kunsten, Antwerp, TL; M.E.P.L., TR. 37 The Granger Collection. 38 *Japanese Kimono for a Woman*, late 18th century, Victoria & Albert Museum, London, TL; Courtesy Laurie Platt Winfrey, TR, BR. 39 *Weariness*, *c.* 1879-1880, drawing by Constantin Meunier, Musées Royaux des Beaux-Arts de Belgique, Musée Constantin Meunier, Brussels. 40 *A Coal Mine with Steam Winding Engine and Cart-Weighing Machine*, *c.*1820, anonymous painting, National Museums & Galleries on Merseyside, Walker Art Gallery, Liverpool. 41 S.M., TL; *Coal Waggon* from L'Art d'Exploiter les Mines de Charbon de Terre, 1768-76 by Jean Morand, BR. 43 Bildarchiv Preussischer Kulturbesitz. 44 *Miners going Home from the Mine*, painting by Constantin Meunier, Musées Royaux des Beaux-Arts de Belgique, Musée Constantin Meunier, Brussels. 45 *Truck in the Mine*, *c.* 1890, painting by Constantin Meunier, Musées Royaux des Beaux-Arts de Belgique, Musée Constantin Meunier, Brussels. 46 Arthur Lockwood. 47 The Historical Society of Schuylkill County, Pottsville, Pa., TR; The George Bretz Collection, Albin O. Kuhn Library, University of Maryland, Baltimore County, BL. 48 S.M., TL; Range/Bettmann, TR. 49 T.B.A. 50 Illustration by Kate Simunek, BL; *The Cobbler*, painting by Jan Miel, Northampton Museums and Art Gallery, BM; *Manfield's Closing Room, Northampton*, *c.*1900, B.S.C. Footwear Supplies Limited, BR. 51 Courtesy Laurie Platt Winfrey. 52 William Morris Gallery, London, BL; *Portrait of William Morris*, by Emery Walker, St Bride Printing Library, BR. 53 Pages from the Merton Abbey Dye Book, 1882-91, Berger Collection, Carmel, California, TL; William Morris Gallery, London, ML, MR. 54 *Sweatshop in Ludlow Street Tenement*, *c.*1889, photograph by Jacob A. Riis, Museum of the City of New York, TR; Detail from photograph, *Woman carrying take-home Piecework*, photograph by Lewis W. Hine, International Museum of Photography at George Eastman House, ML. 55 Sevres, Christie's, London/ B.A.L., M; M.E.P.L., B. 56 E.T.A., TR; John Gorman, from Banner Bright, *An Illustrated History of Trade Union Banners*, John Gorman, Scorpion Publishing Ltd, 1986, ML; M.E.P.L., BR. 57 T.B.A. 58 The Mansell Collection,TL; TUC/T.B.A., BR. 59, 60 Leicester Museums and Art Gallery, photograph by S.W.A. Newton, 1890s. 61 M.E.P.L., TL; *Maid Descending Stairs*, 1875, watercolour by Albert Goodwin, Museum of London, TR; Range/Bettmann, BL. 62 Henkel & Cie, Dusseldorf, ML; AEG-Telefunken, Braunschweig, B. 63 M.E.P.L., TL; *Choosing The Wedding Gown*, painting by William Mulready, Victoria & Albert Museum, London/E.T.A., BR. 64 Roger-Viollet, T, BL, BR. 65 Museum of London BL; M.E.P.L., BR. 66 Cambridgeshire Libraries. 67 *The Crèche*, 1890, painting by Albert Anker, Oskar Reinhart Foundation, Winterthur. 68 *The Birth*, painting by Victor Lecomte, Musée des Beaux-Arts, Nantes/Giraudon, MR; M.E.P.L., BL. 69 *The Crèche For Orphaned Children*, painting by J.H. Marlet, Musée De L'Assistance Publique -Hopitaux de Paris/Giraudon, TR; *Leaving The Maternity Ward*, painting by A. Desmarest, Musée De L'Assistance Publique-Hopitaux de Paris/Giraudon, MR; M.E.P.L., BL, BR. 70 Strathclyde Regional Archive, TL; M.E.P.L., TR. 71 M.E.P.L., TL; *Behind The Bar*, 1882, watercolour by J.H. Henshall, Museum of London, TR; Range/ Bettmann, BR. 72 M.E.P.L., BL; T.B.A., BR. 73 Range/Bettmann, TL; *A Child's Funeral*, 1879, painting by Albert Edelfelt, Ateneumiin taide museo, Helsinki, B. 74 Ullstein Bilderdienst, MR; Roger-Viollet, B. 75 *Poor on the Steps of the Ara Coeli, Rome*, Pinacoteca Di Brera/Alinari/ Giraudon. 76 M.E.P.L.,TR; T.B.A., BL; Robert Opie Collection, BR. 77 A.G.K., London, TL; Robert Opie Collection, MM; T.B.A., MR; Library of Congress, B. 78 T.B.A., T; Birmingham City Libraries/ T.B.A., BL; S.M., BR. 79 *Queue at the Bakery*, painting by C.A. Andrieux, Musee Carnavalet/Giraudon, T; T.B.A., MR. 80 Portsmouth Athenaeum, TR; Courtesy of Society For The Preservation Of New England Antiquities, ML; *Reverend John Atwood and His Family*, *c.* 1870, painting by H.F. Darby, The Museum Of Fine Arts, Boston, Gift of Maxim Karolik to the M. and M. Karolik Collection of American Paintings, B. 81 T.B.A., TR, BL. 82 M.E.P.L., TL. 82 Musée des Arts Decoratifs, Paris/T.B.A., TL, Harlingue-Viollet, BL, BR. 84-85 Illustration by Terence Dalley. 86 By kind permission of Cadbury Limited/T.B.A., TL, TM. 87 M.E.P.L., TR, BL; Courtesy of Unilever/T.B.A., MR. 88 *Saying Grace at Grandmother's Birthday*, 1893, painting by J.H. Lorimer, Musée D'Orsay, Paris/ Lauros-Giraudon, TL; *Poor People*, painting by A. Collin, Musée Des Beaux-Arts, Tournai/Giraudon, TR. 89 M.E.P.L., T; Cassella Farbwerke, Frankfurt/Main, B. 90 *Sympathy with the Poor*, 1886, painting by M. Roy, Musée Des Beaux-Arts et D'Archeologie, Rennes/Giraudon, TL; *A Lunch Party, South Africa*, photograph by Horace W. Nicholls, The Royal Photographic Society, Bath, TR. 91 *Farthing Breakfasts*, 1880, The Salvation Army. 92 BASF, Ludwigshafen. 93 *Sketch of the Boulevard de Montmartre*, 1877, painting by A. Gill, Musée Carnavalet/ Giraudon. 94 *Pietro Learning to Write*, photograph by Jacob A. Riis, Museum of the City of New York, TL; *Portrait of the Artist's Mother, Brother and Sister*, painting by L.J.F. Bonnat, Musee Bonnat/ Giraudon, TR. 95 Photograph by Donald McLeish/R.H.P.L., ML; *Happy Family*, painting by A.H. Dargelas, Wolverhampton Art Gallery/Bx-Giraudon. 96 E.T.A., TR; The Illustrated London News Picture Library, B. 97 Musée Carnavalet/Lauros-Giraudon. 98 Daily Citizen, 2 July 1863, Felix Farley's Bristol Journal, 9 April 1814, British Library, London. 99 T.B.A. 100 *Medicin for the Poor*, painting by J. Leonard, Muée Des Beaux-Arts, Valenciennes/Lauros-Giraudon. 101 Arthur Lockwood, ML; E.T.A., BR. 102 M.E.P.L., TL; *Visiting Day At The Hospital*, 1889, painting by H.J.J. Geoffroy, Hotel De Ville/Lauros-Giraudon, TR. 103 M.E.P.L. 104 T.B.A. 105 T.B.A., TM, BR; Sunderland and Museum & Art Gallery (Tyne and Wear Museum), ML. 106 From *A Bio-Bibliography of Edward Jenner*, by W.R. Lefanu, published by Harvey and Blythe Ltd, 1951. 107 Arthur Lockwood, TL; *Gas-Works at Courcelles*, 1884, painting by E.J. Detahaye, Musée Du Petit-Palais, Paris/Lauros-Giraudon, B. 108 *Reflexions of a Hungry Man*, 1894, E. Longoni, Musee Civico, Biella/Alinari/ Giraudon. 109 The Granger Collection, BL; T.B.A., BM; Boyer-Viollet, BR. 110 E.T.A. 111 Range/Bettmann, TL; The Granger Collection, TM; T.B.A., TR; M.E.P.L., B. 112 Royal Collection © HM The Queen, Queen Elizabeth II, T; A.K.G., London. ML, B. 113 *The Jerry McAuley Mission*, 1897, Museum of the City of New York. 114 M.E.P.L., TL; *Slum Sisters visiting a poor Family*, *c.* 1890, The Salvation Army. 115 *Elephant & Castle*, 1912, Hulton-Deutsch. 116 Range/Bettmann. 117 Tower Hamlets Public Library. 118 The Granger Collection, TL; Range/ Bettmann. 119 *The Barracks, Mott Street between Bleecker and Houston Streets*, photograph by Jacob A. Riis, Diagram of evolution of Tenement, Museum of the City of New York. 120 Ullstein Bilderdienst, BL; M.E.P.L., BR. 121 Arthur Lockwood, TL; Currie & Ives, 1884 colour lithograph, Metropolitan Museum of Art, New York, Schenkung A.S. Colgate/T.B.A., TR. 122 Deutsches Museum München, TL; *Inside The Omnibus*, 1880, painting by M. Delondre, Musée Carnavalet, Paris/Giraudon, B. 123 *The Opening of the South Docks, Sunderland*, 1850, painting by Mark Thompson, Sunderland Museum & Art Gallery (Tyne and Wear Museums), ML; Brunel University Library, MR. 124 From the Illustrated Australian News, October 1880, State Library of Victoria, Melbourne. 125 M.E.P.L., T; *Police Dormitory, West 47 Street*, 1890s, photograph by Jacob A.Riis, Museum of the City of New York, B. 126 Hulton-Deutsch.127 T.B.A., TL, TR; M.E.P.L., B. 128-9 Illustration by Paul Wright. 130 Range/Bettmann. 131 *The Song of the Shirt*, 1902, painting by Albert Rutherston, Bradford Art Galleries and Museums/B.A.L., TL; *In the Morning Room*, *c.*1905, painting by William Rothenstein/© Manchester City Art Galleries, TR. 132 *A Bloomsbury Family*, 1907, painting by William Orpen, Scottish National Gallery of Modern Art/B.A.L., TL; Range/Bettmann, MR; Library of Congress, BL. 133 The Granger Collection, ML; M.E.P.L., MR. 134 *The Old Servant*, 1884, painting by L.H.M. Frederic, Musée D'Orsay, Paris/Lauros-Giraudon, TL; *The Laundress*, painting by A.D. Gautier, Musée Des Beaux-Arts, Caen/Giraudon, TR. 135 Ullstein Bilderdienst. 136 Hulton-Deutsch, BL; Roger-Viollet, BR. 137 *Le Chalet du Cycle au Bois de Boulogne*, *c.*1900, painting by J. Beraud, SPADEM/Bulloz. 138 *Sylvia Pankhurst addressing a Crowd*, 1912, Museum of London, T; Range/Bettmann, BL. 139 M.E.P.L. 140 *Street Musicians, King Street, Greenwich*, 1884, Greenwich Public Library, T; *Hampstead Fair*, photograph by Paul Martin, T.B.A., B. 141 Staples & Charles Ltd., Washington D.C., from, *Fairground Art: The Art Forms Of Travelling Fairs, Carousels and Carnival Midways* by Geoff Weedon and Richard Ward, published by White Mouse Editions Ltd./New Cavendish Books, 1981, T; New York Historical Society, Sammlung Bella C. Landauer, MR. 142 *Dancing Bear*, photograph by Paul Martin/ Hulton-Deutsch. TL; T.B.A., M; *Boulevard des Capucines and the Vaudeville Theatre*, painting by J. Beraud, Christie's, London/B.A.L./Giraudon/ ADAGP. 143 P.T. *Barnum and Commodore Nutt*, photography by Gurney, *c.*1863, Becker Collection, Syracuse University, TM; Robert Opie Collection, BR. 144 *Beer Festival*, 1886, painting by J.M. Hupfer, Private Collection,Bildarchiv Preussischer Kulturbesitz/Giraudon, TL; T.B.A., TR. 145 M.E.P.L. 146 T.B.A., ML; Thomas Cook Travel Archive, MR. 147 T.B.A., MR, BL; *A Game of Croquet*, painting by Winslow Homer, Private Collection/ B.A.L., BR. 148 *Popular Music-Hall Song Sheet*, 1870s, British Museum, London, TL; *The Old Bedford*, *c.*1895, painting by Walter Sickert, Board of Trustees of The National Museums And Galleries on Merseyside (Walker Art Gallery, Liverpool), TR. 149 Bibliothèque Nationale, Paris, BL, BR. 150 M.E.P.L., TL, MM; E.T.A., TR; *No.10 Fish Street Hill East, City of London*, 1802, Survey drawing by John Baker, British Architectural Library, RIBA Drawings Collection, BL; Meissen, *c.*1748, Antique Porcelain Company, London/ B.A.L., BR. 151 *Miniature of Catherine The Great*, Imperial Porcelain, Hermitage, St Petersburg/B.A.L., TL; E.T.A., TM; Musée Carnavalet, Paris/Lauros-Giraudon, TR; M.E.P.L., ML, BR; The Mansell Collection, BL. 152 M.E.P.L., TM, ML, BM; E.T.A., TR; S.M., BL; Arthur Lockwood, BR. 153 Bildarchiv d. Ost. Nationalbibliothek, TL; E.T.A.,TR; Thomas Cook Travel Archive, ML; M.E.P.L., MR, BR; Welbeck Golin/ Harris Communications Limited, BL. 154 M.E.P.L., TL, The Mansell Collection, TR; The Wimbledon Lawn Tennis Museum, ML, MR; Marylebone Cricket Club, MM; From, Puck. March 17, 1886, BL; Culver Pictures Inc., BR. 155 M.E.P.L., TL, BL; Photograph by Arnold Genthe, Palace of The Legion of Honor, TM; Range/Bettmann, TR, MR; Culver Pictures Inc., BR.

Front cover: Arthur Lockwood, TL; Courtesy of Society for the Preservation of New England Antiquities, ML; Hulton Deutsch, MM, BM; Robert Opie Collection, TR, BM; T.B.A., BL; The Sutcliffe Gallery, Whitby/T.B.A., BR.

Back cover: S.M., TL; M.E.P.L., TR, BM; From the trade catalogue of Silber & Fleming, *c.* 1880s, ML, MR; Ullstein Bilderdienst, BL.

59-007-2